Beer is so much more than a drink, it is a pleasure-giving, thirst-quenching, heart-warming blend of art and alchemy, of passion and precision. A profession for some and a fascination for others, beer is brewed, enjoyed and celebrated the World over. It offers a greater diversity of taste and style than any other beverage and has a history that can be traced back to the earliest human civilisations.

Alex Barlow

Written by Alex Barlow & Diane Barlow.

Edited by Diane Barlow.

First edition published by red apple pmc limited in 2008. PO Box 4431, Sheffield, S10 9DS.

Design by red apple pmc limited and Curve Digital Limited.

Artwork, illustrations and reprographics by Curve Digital Limited except where otherwise acknowledged on p.171.

Food & Drink photography by Curve Digital Limited.

Other photography courtesy of A&D Barlow and Curve Digital Limited, unless stated otherwise.

ISBN 978-0-9559992-0-8

A CIP catalogue record is available from the British Library.

Printed in the UK on FSC and PEFC certified, chlorine-free papers, produced in mills certified to ISO 14001.

CONTENTS

BEER OFFERS A GREATER DIVERSITY OF TASTE AND STYLE THAN ANY OTHER BEVERAGE AND HAS A HISTORY THAT CAN BE TRACED BACK TO THE EARLIEST HUMAN CIVILISATIONS. TODAY, BEER IS STILL A GREAT UNIFIER, A DRINK ENJOYED BY MEN AND WOMEN, YOUNG AND OLD, RICH AND POOR ACROSS ALL THE CONTINENTS. IT IS A GREAT, REFRESHING, ALCOHOLIC DRINK; THE BEST LOVED LONG DRINK IN THE WORLD.

Beer is the most diverse alcoholic drink too, with dozens of different styles, thousands of different breweries and tens of thousands of beer brands. There is something to appeal to everyone. During my 25 years in the brewing industry I have brewed, marketed, sold and talked about beer for a living in the UK and internationally. Beer is my profession and *my passion*. Over recent years I have created and presented beer style and flavour events for many hundreds of people, from many different backgrounds, including audiences from the beer industry, retailing, media and the general public.

This page: Photos: www.antoniogoard.com
The Times newspaper, event

Opposite: Photos: www.andyfallon.co.uk
Arena magazine event

I always need to go *back to basics* about what beer is and what styles and flavours are out there. By giving people new skills and the confidence to make beer choices that suit them, they leave having had a great time and with a new respect for beer. I hope this experience pack does the same for you.

The ALL **BEER** GUIDE provides an unrivalled experience, the ultimate laymans guide to beer styles and their flavours. Whether you prefer Lager or Ale, popular or speciality beers, this guide will suit the novice and enthusiast alike.

It is divided into 6 easy-to-use guides with unique tools for the job:

ALL **BEER STYLES** Beer families and the top 25 styles

ALL **BEER BREWING** Brewing in flavour

ALL **BEER EXPERIENCE** Sense it!

ALL **BEER FLAVOURS** Flavours of the 25 top beer styles

ALL **BEER SKILLS** How to judge a beer

ALL **BEER ANSWERS** Is this beer off?

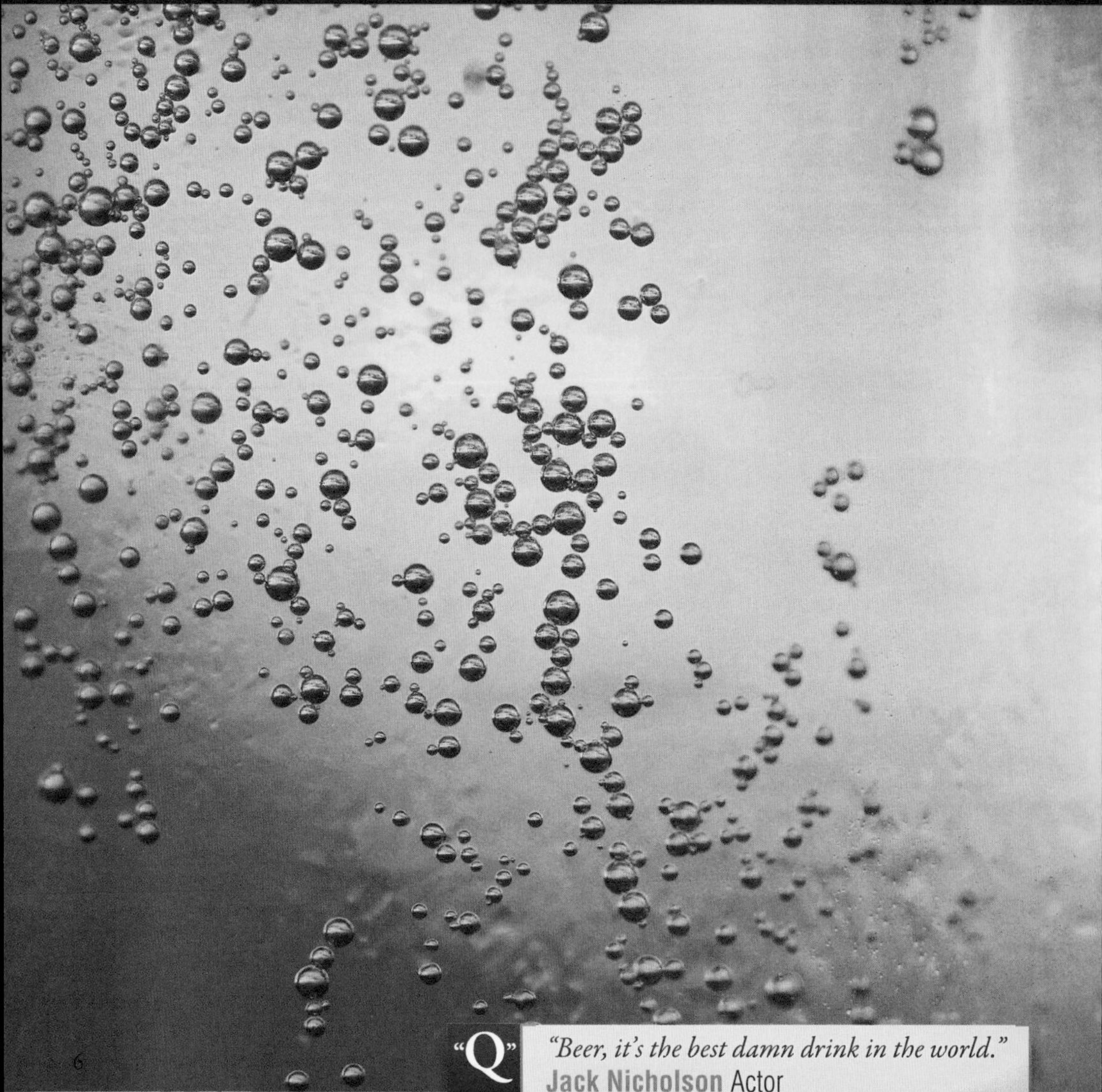

"Q" *"Beer, it's the best damn drink in the world."*
Jack Nicholson Actor

Working together with the ALL BEER EXPERIENCE PACK, the ALL BEER GUIDE is much more than an introduction to beer styles and flavours. They contain all you need to start getting your head around the different beers available today, to build your skills, know your preferences, and tell a good beer from a bad one.

Ten ALL BEER INTERACTIVE (**AB*i***) sections give you 'hands on' experience of the flavour discovery exercises I use in live events. You can check your experiences against mine in the reference section. The **AB*i's*** include genuine brewers malts and a specially developed hop aroma card. To familiarise yourself with the most common beer flavours you can use the list of common store cupboard items on page 168.

'ALL BEER' DOESN'T JUST TELL YOU WHAT IT'S LIKE,

WE LET YOU EXPERIENCE IT FOR YOURSELF!

The ALL BEER FLAVOURMAX tasting glass enhances the flavour experience of any beer you try. 'How to judge a beer' allows you to compare your thoughts on six well-known beers with ours, using the *flavour notepad* and *flavour reference cards*. Our jargon-busting Glossary will explain all those brewing terms too.

This ultimate easy-to-use beer flavour and style guide will cut the mystery, helping you identify your own flavour *preferences* and choose beers you will like. I hope you enjoy using this pack and share your experiences and feedback with us at www.allbeer.co.uk. Enjoy.

Alex

Alex Barlow – Master Brewer

A WORLD OF CHOICE

PALE ALE, AMERICAN LIGHT LAGER, BEST BITTER, STOUT, WEIZEN, KÖLSCH, MILD, OLD ALE, DARK LAGER, BARLEY WINE, SPECIAL BITTER, OUD BRUIN, CZECH PILSNER, FARO, CONTINENTAL PILSENER, BOCK, LAMBIC, BIER DE GARDE, DUNKEL, GUEUZE, PORTER, HELLES, FRUIT BEER, SPECIAL BELGES, BROWN ALE, SCOTCH ALE, ABBEY, BLONDE ALE, WEISSE, TRAPPIST, MÄRZEN, AMBER LAGER, IPA, SAISON, OKTOBERFEST, WITTE, SUMMER ALE.

SPOILED FOR CHOICE

Beer culture has spread from the ancient brewing civilisations of Egypt and Mesopotamia to Europe, influenced over time by cultural development, evolution and agriculture, religion and the industrial revolution.

As populations migrated, brewers from Western Europe started breweries in North and Central America. Then American brewers started breweries in the Far East, taking and *adapting beer styles* as they went.

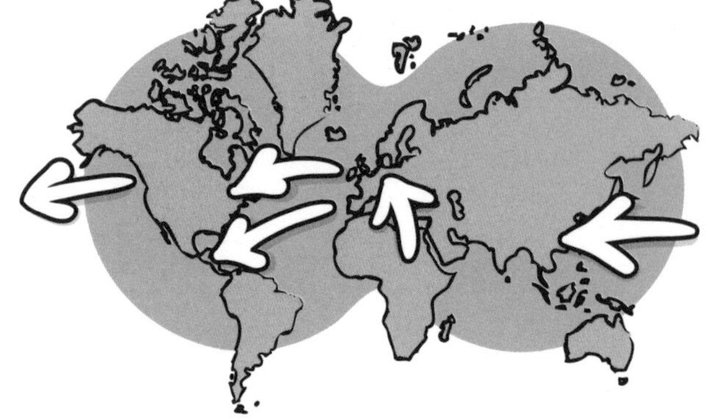

More recently, technical innovation, experimentation and *consumer trends* reshaped traditional brewing boundaries, re-inventing beers and blurring the distinctions between different beer styles. Continuing global development and increasingly *cosmopolitan lifestyles* have resulted in a huge breadth of beer styles and flavours from across the World becoming ever more widely available.

This growing appetite for new and different beers, a powerful retail sector and a flourishing micro-brewing industry have ensured that, for *sheer diversity* and range of choice, there is nowhere better than the UK.

"Fermentation and civilization are inseparable."
John Ciardi Poet

In the UK, the average supermarket stocks *between 100 and 200 beer brands*, most pubs and bars stock at least 12 draught and packaged beers. Whether doing the shopping or in the pub, do you just tend to stick to what you know, the beers you are familiar with?

The beer layout in supermarkets often doesn't help you to distinguish between different beer styles. For example, Stella Artois, Carling and Budweiser may be placed next to each other, despite the fact they are different styles of Lager, namely: Continental Pilsener, Helles and American Light with *totally different tastes.*

The ALL BEER GUIDE will de-mystify 25 beer styles and give you the skill and confidence to choose beers that suit your taste.

Worldwide, beer outsells wine everywhere except France, Italy and Bulgaria REF#1

WHAT'S YOUR STYLE? BLONDE, BRUN or DARK?

Beer styles? Beer's beer and Lager's Lager isn't it?
Well no. It's not as simple as that

BEER IS THE COLLECTIVE NAME FOR ALCOHOLIC BEVERAGES FERMENTED FROM GRAINS AND FLAVOURED WITH HOPS

So, Lagers are light coloured and Ales are darker?

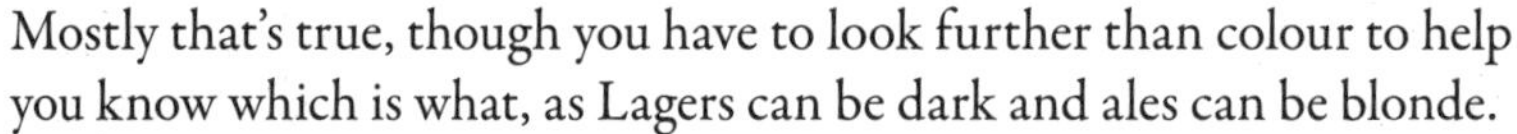

Mostly that's true, though you have to look further than colour to help you know which is what, as Lagers can be dark and ales can be blonde.

What about the ingredients?
Checking the ingredients lists won't help you either, as many will list the same four main ingredients.

What about serving temperature, Lagers are served cold and Ales 'warm', aren't they?
Well no, because Wheat beers and Kölsch are ales despite the pale colour, lighter taste and chilled serve.

So how do we distinguish between beer styles?
To start with, beer is sub-divided into 3 distinct families:

Ales + Lagers + Lambics = ALL BEER

"Q" *"Afraid of the dark, Lagerboy?"*
Hobgoblin beer campaign UK

The main distinction between the *beer families* is the yeast-type used and how it ferments. More about the flavour differences later.

ALES use cultured Ale yeast strains, which *ferment* at *warmer* temperatures, and tend to collect on top of the beer after fermentation (top-fermenting).

LAGERS use cultured Lager yeast strains, which *ferment* at *cooler* temperatures, and tend sink to the bottom after fermentation (bottom-fermenting).

LAMBIC beers are fermented at warm temperatures using *wild* (non-cultured) yeast and bacteria from the surrounding environment. Yes, they leave the window open and see what floats in! These often don't settle, so the beer is cloudy.

Adding fruits to the fermentation can produce some *fantastic flavours*, while adding more unusual ingredients such as smoked malt, herbs, spices and even chillies can create other unique characteristics. However, they are all variants on Ale, Lager or Lambic styles.

The ALL BEER STYLE GUIDE (overleaf) places the 25 most popular beer styles into the 3 beer family groups. Later on we'll introduce the ALL BEER FLAVOUR GUIDE, which defines the flavour characteristics of those 25 styles.

Yeasts are microscopic, single-cell organisms. Their latin name, Saccharomyces literally means sugar-eating fungus.

Each beer style sits within its typical colour range.

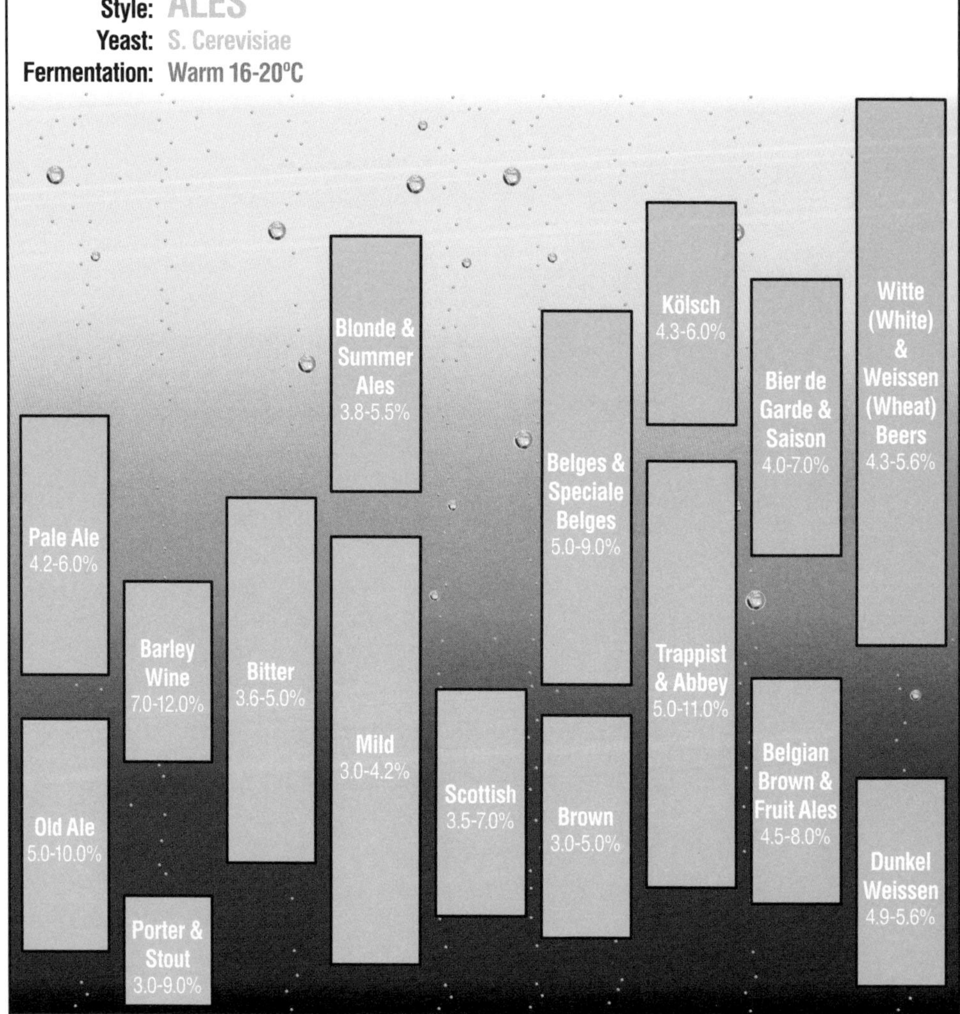

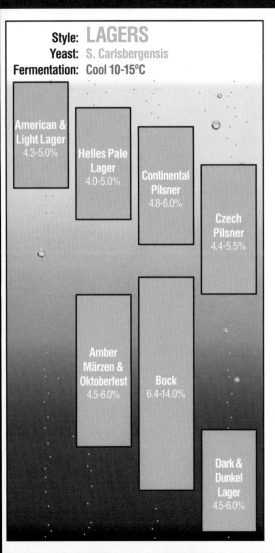

Style: LAGERS
Yeast: S. Carlsbergensis
Fermentation: Cool 10-15°C

American & Light Lager 4.3-5.0%

Helles Pale Lager 4.0-5.0%

Continental Pilsner 4.8-6.0%

Czech Pilsner 4.4-5.5%

Amber Märzen & Oktoberfest 4.5-6.0%

Bock 6.4-14.0%

Dark & Dunkel Lager 4.5-6.0%

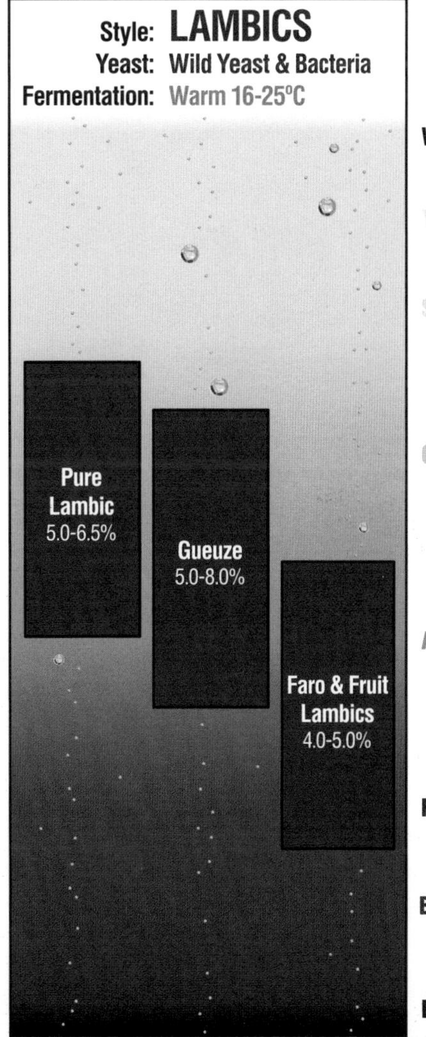

WHITE
YELLOW
STRAW
GOLD
AMBER
RUBY
BROWN
BLACK

For guidance only

BUILDING BLOCKS OF FLAVOUR

4 simple, natural ingredients form the building blocks of beer flavour:

Pure Water

Malted Barley

Hop Flowers

Brewers Yeast

NATURALLY VERSATILE

Does beer have any articial flavours, colours and preservatives? It shouldn't. Beer doesn't really need them, as alcohol and hops provide natural preservative and anti-bacterial properties.

The natural raw materials are the building blocks of an impressive range of *flavours* from citrus and apples to caramel and chocolate, and a spectrum of *colours*, from cloudy white, through lustrous gold and amber, to darkest black.

An astounding range of colours and flavours can be achieved with just these four, however brewers have access to other materials too. Sources of starch or sugar other than barley malt can moderate malt flavour or introduce flavours of their own, creating unique and characteristic differences. (page 32)

"Q"

"He was a wise man who invented beer."
Plato Philosopher

PURE WATER

Water makes up around 95% of your beer, dependent upon its alcohol content. The water used in brewing has an important effect on the way the beer tastes and feels in your mouth, created by the minerals naturally dissolved in the water.

The mineral levels change from area to area, so certain waters are suitable for brewing certain beer styles. That is why Plzen and Munich are the natural homes of light and dark Lagers respectively, Dublin became the spiritual home of Stout, and Burton-on-Trent was the capital of Pale Ale brewing.

#1 – WATER

Compare the taste of your tap water to a couple of common mineral waters from different regions.

Most people can pick up some differences.

Compare your interactive experiences with our **ABi** notes on pages 162-167.

CITY	Plzen CR	Golden Colorado US	Birmingham UK	Burton-on-Trent UK	Dublin Ireland
Liquor character	very soft	very soft	medium hard	hard	very hard
Main salts	low	low	high chloride	high calcium, sulphate, some bicarbonate	high bicarbonate
Flavour impact	very soft	soft & smooth	sweet, smooth	chalky & astringent	alkaline, drying
Typical beers	balanced pilsners	light lagers	soft milds	structured ales	definitive stouts

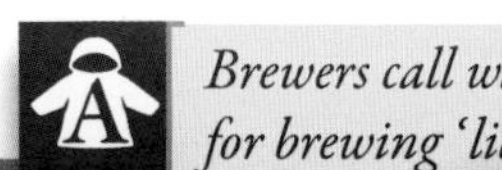

Brewers call water for brewing 'liquor'.

MALTED BARLEY

Barley is the cereal crop most widely used for brewing. Its low protein levels help ensure that beer is clear and bright, it also provides the *sugars* for fermenting beer, in the same way that grape juices provide the sugars for fermenting wine. Over 2000 *grains* of malted barley are used in every pint.

Unlike grapes, *barley has to be malted* to develop the sugars, colour, flavour and body it brings to the beer. Malting combines 3 processes:

Steeping – *wetting* the barley grain so it starts to grow

Germination – *sprouting* the grain until rootlets appear

Kilning – *drying* the green malt in a kiln, developing colour and flavour

A dozen or more styles of malt can be created by varying the barley selection and the time, temperature and conditions of germination and kilning.

"This is grain, which any fool can eat, but for which the Lord intended a more divine means of consumption... beer!"
Friar Tuck in Robin Hood Prince of Thieves

THE BREWERS TALENT

The art of the brewer is to select and combine the relevant malt types to create distinctive and characteristic malt-derived flavours, which balance and harmonise with those from their chosen hops and yeast.

In most beers, the majority of the final colour and sweetness is derived from the selected malts, which are dissolved in the liquor during the early stages of brewing to form a sugary solution called wort.

#2 – MALT

The ALL BEER EXPERIENCE pack contains unmalted Barley and 4 common brewing malts:
Pilsner Lager, Pale Ale, Crystal and Chocolate.

1. Starting with the Barley, pour some into your palm, rub hard with your thumb, then take a sniff. Is there a distinctive aroma?
2. Take 1 or 2 grains and chew on them. (**WARNING:** Barley is very hard!) How would you describe the taste and the way it feels in your mouth?
3. Try each malt in turn. How do they compare to barley?
4. What are the most noticeable flavours of each malt?

The word 'Ale' derives from the word for sorcery or magic, a reference to the 'magical' process that turns the sweet, malty wort into beer. REF#2

MALT Typical flavour contributions

MALT TYPE	BEER TYPE	COLOUR IMPACT
PALE PILSNER	Lagers	
PALE ALE	Ales	
CRYSTAL	Ales, Amber and Dark Lagers	
CHOCOLATE	Ales, Stouts, Dark Lagers	

BEER FLAVOUR IMPACT

HOP FLOWERS

The hop is a climbing plant, cultivated and used for brewing in Europe since at least the first millennia. Hops are like the brewer's herbs and spices, there are a host of different varieties, each with their own flavour attributes. Depending upon the beer style, between *1 and 4 hop cones* may be used per pint.

The hop cone is the flower of the plant and is harvested for the precious *lupulin* glands nestled at the base of the petals. They contain *sticky resins* that bring a balancing bitterness to the sweet malt sugars, and aromatic oils, whose aroma qualities vary from one hop variety to another.

Like herbs or spices hops are *better* the *fresher* they are. Would a Bolognese be better with freshly chopped basil and oregano leaves or dried herbs from that jar in the back of the cupboard, that has been open for 2 years? Hops become rapidly oxidised, losing bitterness and aroma, if they are left open to the air. So brewers buy their hops compressed into vacuum-packed foil blocks, like fresh ground coffee, to protect the valuable resins and oils.

Hops help preserve beer flavour too, as the same resins that make beer bitter have an anti-bacterial effect on organisms that can send beer 'off'.

"Q"

"A little bit of beer is divine medicine."
Paracelus Greek Physician

DRAMATIC AROMATICS

The options on hop use are almost endless. Some brewers use single varieties to great effect, others blend for bitter and aromatic qualities. Lambic brewers age their hops to eliminate the bitterness and fresh aromas, leaving only natural antibacterial protection and mature cheesy notes. Mmm!?

Timing the hop addition has a major effect on the final beer aroma. Hops for bitterness are added at the start of the boiling process, hops for *aroma* can be added at the end of boil or later in the brewing process, for greater impact and layering of flavour.

ABi

#3 – HOPS

We have micro-encapsulated oils from three distinctive hop varieties, to demonstrate their unique aromas. The aroma patches may be used several times.

1. Taking the Hop Card, scratch one patch and take gentle, shallow sniffs.
2. Scratch and sniff the other hop oil patches in turn.
3. What are the main aromas of each one? Notice any differences?
4. Scratch two together and smell the combined effect.

Hops are related to cannabis. They don't possess the psychoactive effect of cannabinol, but they are soporific.

HOPS Typical flavour contributions

HOP VARIETY	BEER TYPE	USED FOR
FUGGLES	Ales	Aroma
NORTHDOWN	Ales & Lager	Bitterness & Aroma
STYRIAN GOLDINGS	Ales & Lager	Bitterness & Aroma
SAAZ	Lager	Mainly Aroma

BEER FLAVOUR IMPACT

BREWERS YEAST

Yeast is the single-cell fungus brewers use to ferment wort and create beer. Fermentation is the natural process of the yeast *eating and reproducing*. As it does, it absorbs malt sugars and nutrients from the wort and *excretes* what it doesn't need. Conveniently for us, that includes alcohol, carbon dioxide and up to 1000 different *flavour-active substances*. The range of flavours varies from yeast to yeast, but it takes the contribution of around 34 billion cells to make 1 pint!

Most brewers have their own *pet yeast strains* genetically fingerprinted, and store pure cultures under liquid nitrogen at a chilly -196°C. Periodically they grow up a fresh culture to replace yeast that's tired of reproducing. Each yeast strain has its own *individual style*, doing things its own way and producing distinctive flavour results.

Some brewers use a common strain for all their beers, others a different strain for each brand, while some mix strains of 2, 3 or more yeasts. Multiple yeasts can act in concert to produce *layered flavours* and more complex and challenging beers. Other brewers purposely select yeasts that only produce a limited range of flavours, creating simpler, easy-drinking and more refreshing beers.

"A meal of bread, cheese and beer constitutes the chemically perfect food."
Queen Elizabeth I

FLAVOUR CREATOR

The flavour-active compounds yeast produces are similar to those that give other naturally occurring substances their *distinctive flavours* and aromas. Professional tasters use over 100 recognised flavour descriptors, some with very technical names. However, many of the groups of flavours produced can be described in more everyday language.

Yeast creates up to *half the flavour* of the finished beer. For most beers it does it's job and is removed from the finished product by filtration. Exceptions to this are cask Ales, Wheat, Lambic and bottle-conditioned beers that are unfiltered, un-pasteurised and are seen as *'live' beers.*

ABi

#4 – YEAST

Yeast is removed from the great majority of beers to make them clear and bright. So, yeast itself isn't part of the final flavour experience.
To experience the taste of brewers yeast you could:

1. Taste the sediment from a bottle of wheat or bottle-conditioned beer.
2. Taste Marmite, which is highly concentrated and cooked brewers yeast.

Each yeast cell reproduces up to 5 times during fermentation. So the brewer gets more yeast out than he puts in. The nutritious excess yeast is used to make Marmite.

YEAST Aroma contributions

BEER FLAVOUR IMPACT

SWEETS

SULPHURY COMPOUNDS

FRESH FRUITS

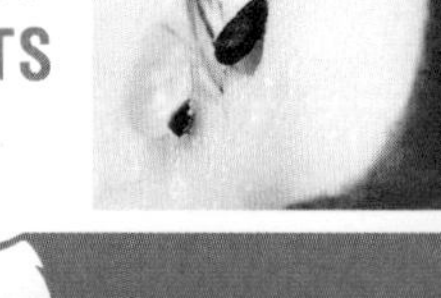

ALCOHOLS

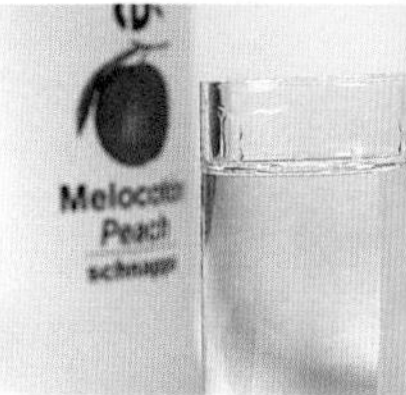

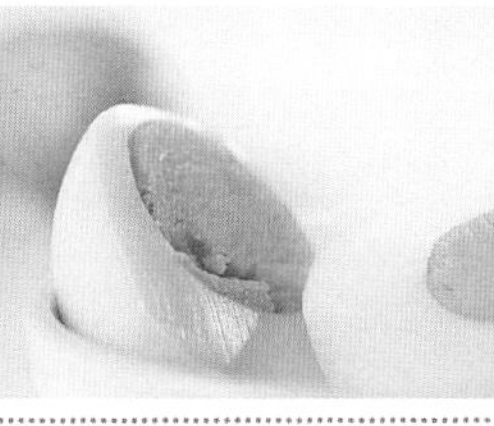

DRIED OR PRESERVED FRUITS

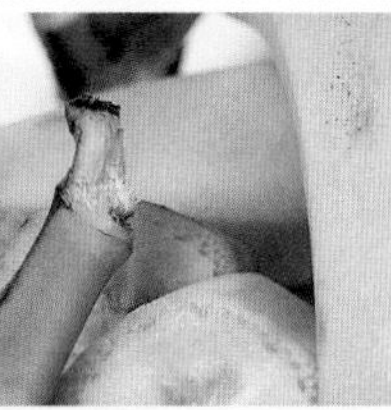

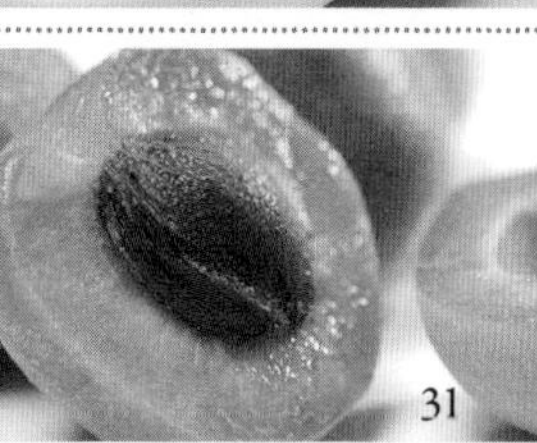

OTHER INGREDIENTS

In the UK and much of Western Europe the main beer styles use either exclusively or a majority of barley malt, because good quality malting barley is readily available. Alternative cereal grains or syrups that provide sources of fermentable sugar are termed 'adjuncts'. Brewers may use adjuncts for a number of reasons:

Flavour – To produce a different beer style.
e.g. Wheat beer replaces 30-70% of barley malt with wheat.

Financial – Sugar syrups or other grains may help increase brewing efficiency, or be a cheaper alternative to malted barley.

Availability – To produce beers using materials that are more readily available locally. e.g. maize in the America's; rice in the Far East; sorghum in Africa.

SUGAR SOURCE	Colour impact	Flavour impact	Other effects
Sugar syrup	reduces colour	reduces flavour	none
Rice	reduces colour	reduces flavour	reduces body
Maize	reduces colour	crisper taste	can give oily, rancid aroma
Wheat	little change	medicinal & bubblegum	cloudy, improves head
Oats	reduces colour	smoother	cloudy
Rye	darker	spicy & drying	none
Sorghum	darker	bitter taste	cloudy
Fruits (various)	picks up fruit colour	picks up fruit flavour	increases acidity

"Q"

"The mouth of a perfectly happy man is filled with beer."
Ancient Egyptian Saying

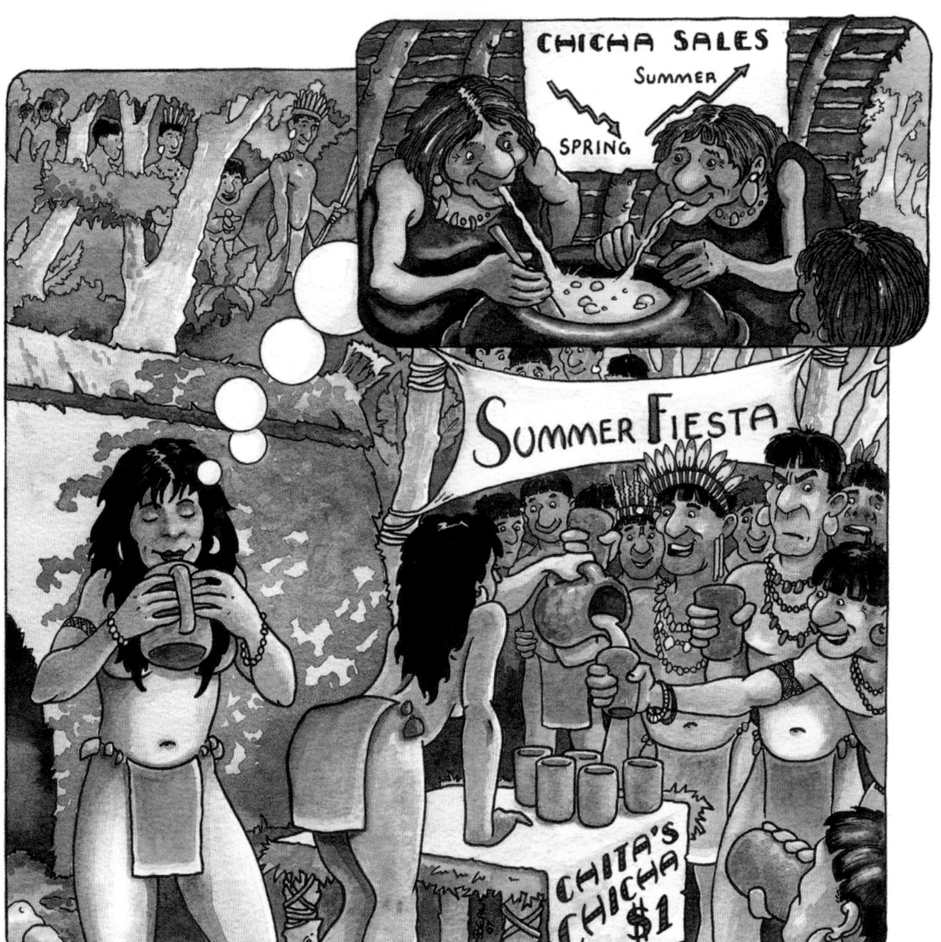

'Chicha' is an ancient beer style, still brewed by South American tribes using the natural enzymes, yeasts and bacteria from the mouths of women, who chew grains, fruits or roots to soften them, then spit them into a pot to ferment.

BEER CHEF'S

Brewing beer is a bit like highly *technical cookery*. With natural ingredients, detailed recipes, hygienic preparation and a combination of skill, flair and technical equipment needed to create all the right flavours.

For consistent beer, brewers need *precise control* of ingredient addition and temperature. They must also master seasonal variations in the hop and barley crops to ensure flavours remain the same.

There's no '*Ready Steady Cook*' for beer though, the quickest processes take around 15 days from malting barley through to drinkable beer, while some premium and speciality beers may be months or years in the making.

photo courtesy of Black Sheep Brewery

"Q"

"Blessing of your heart, you brew good Ale."
William Shakespeare
From Two Gentlemen of Verona

photo courtesy of Black Sheep Brewery

THE BREWERS KITCHEN

Brewing uses some pretty impressive-looking and sounding kit, from 'mash tuns' and 'coppers' to 'hop backs' and 'Yorkshire stone squares'. It may be sleek and sexy with *gleaming coppers* or *brushed steel*, or just plain functional. However, every piece of equipment has an *impact on the flavour* of the finished beer.

BREWING EQUIPMENT AND BEER STYLES

Whilst there are many exceptions, mash tuns and open fermenters are better suited for brewing Ale, double-decoction mashing and cylindro-conical fermenters for brewing Lager.

Unusual equipment and processes can be used to create *unique niche beers*, like the shallow 'cool ships' for cooling and pitching Lambic beer worts, and old oak Sherry or Whiskey casks used for ageing and maturation.

photo courtesy of Black Sheep Brewery

In medieval Britain, brewing was largely the preserve of Monks and women termed 'Ale wives'. Today, a female brewer is called a 'Brewster'.

STAY IN CONTROL

Whatever equipment is used, *accurate* control of time, temperature and yeast is critical. Five minutes too little here, or 2 degrees too much there, can alter beer flavour. Whether the brewery is large or small, automated or manual, good *process control is essential* to create beers of repeatable *high quality.*

Brewers measure, set standards and control quality at each process stage. There can be up to 250 *quality checks* made throughout the brewing process. However, the most important piece of quality control equipment is the *educated palate* of the brewer, who may sample brewing liquor; milled grist; sweet and bittered worts; green, conditioned, bright and packaged beer on a daily basis. That's why a brewer needs a good breakfast!

OUT OF CONTROL

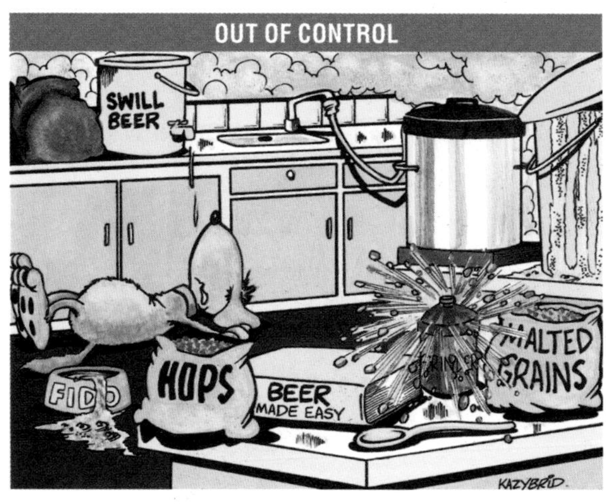

> "Q" *"Ideally, brewers interpret history, and through science they create art."*
> **Don Spencer**
> Silver City Brewery, Washington, USA

STRICT CONTROL

Would you argue with this man?

Unfortunately, I sometimes have to, but I seldom win. Paul Ambler is our Head Brewer; but he's also my Sales Prevention Officer. A few short cuts would allow us to brew and sell more beer. This is the look that prevents me even asking.

All of us at Black Sheep are justifiably proud of our beer, but none more so than Paul.

Paul Theakston
Managing Director

BLACK SHEEP BREWERY

photo courtesy of Black Sheep Brewery UK

The Reinheitsgebot beer purity law of 1516, limiting brewing materials to water, malted barley, hops and yeast, was replaced by the German Beer law in 1993, which also allows wheat malt and sugar use.

Brewing is a succession of batch processes.
The ALL BEER BREWING GUIDE divides it into 10 stages, for convenience, and shows you how those 10 brewing stages impact on *beer flavour development*.

STAGE	1 MALTING	2 MILLING
Process Activity	Germinated and dried barley = MALT HEAT	Crushed malt = GRIST Grist
Time	6-8 days	Up to 1 hour
Temperature	COOL > WARM > HOT	COOL
FLAVOUR IMPACT	Light kilning → grassy/grainy → biscuity → toasted Hot kilning → roasted	Exposes malt flavours

In reality, the process and number of stages vary from brewery to brewery, depending upon the beer styles brewed and the type of equipment they use.

3 MASHING	4 WORT SEPARATION	5 BOILING
Grist + warm water (liquor) = MASH	Mash – grain husks = SWEET WORT	Boiled sweet wort + hops = BITTERED SWEET WORT
Grist		Hops
Up to 3 Hours	Up to 3 Hours	1 to 1.5 hours
WARM	**HOT**	**HOT**
Malt enzymes turn starch to sweet malty sugars	Sweet malty wort solution extracted	Boiling wort increases caramel and toffee-like flavours. Hops add bitterness, floral, fruity and spicy aromas

STAGE	6 TRUB SEPARATION & COOLING	7 FERMENTATION
Process Activity	Removing hop leaves and protein (trub) + chilling = COOLED WORT	Bittersweet wort fermented with yeast = GREEN BEER Yeast
Time	Up to 1 hour	5 to 14 days
Temperature	HOT > COOL	Lagers COOL Ales & Lambics WA
FLAVOUR IMPACT	Some brewers add 'late hops' for extra aroma. Some lager malts can develop vegetable-like aromas	Big flavour impact as fruity and sulphury aromas, alcohol and CO_2 (carbonation) are formed

8 CONDITIONING	9 FILTRATION	10 PACKAGING
Green beer + time = ROUGH BEER	Rough beer − yeast and protein = BRIGHT BEER	Bright beer + containers = PACKAGED BEER
GO TO 10		
3 days to 1 year	1 to 2 hours	1 to 3 hours
VERY COLD	VERY COLD	COLD > HOT > COOL
Flavours mature, carbonation increases	Flavour stabilised by removing yeast, proteins and tannins. Fresh yeast may be added for further maturation in cask or bottle-conditioned beers	Flavour remains stable for stated shelf life. Over-heating or getting air in beer causes stale, papery flavours

PACKAGING AND FLAVOUR

Brewers aim to ensure that at the end of fermentation their beer *tastes excellent* and meets its specified quality standards. However, this beer still has yeast and proteins in, so would not be clear, bright and stable enough to put on a bar or supermarket shelf and meet consumer expectations. Beer still requires 'conditioning' and packaging to become saleable.

Brewers offer consumers a number of ways to purchase and enjoy conditioned beer. Each has pros and cons as regards flavour and '*shelf life*'.

PACKAGE TYPE	Shelf Life	Flavour impact
Cask-conditioned Live yeast remains, or may be filtered then re-seeded with fresh yeast	4-6 weeks	Continues to mature, producing more complex flavours and CO_2. Requires careful, hygienic handling during delivery and in the bar to control CO_2, flavour and clarity or casks are susceptible to infection causing cloudiness and 'off' flavours.
Keg Brewery conditioned, filtered & pasteurised (or sterile filtered)	7-12 weeks	Little change to flavour from brewery conditioning when fresh. Excessive pasteurisation causes cooked flavours and any oxygen picked up causes stale, papery flavours.
Bottle & can Brewery conditioned, filtered & pasteurised (or sterile filtered)	36–52 weeks	Little change to flavour from brewery conditioning when fresh. Excessive pasteurisation causes cooked flavours and any oxygen picked up causes stale, papery flavours.
Bottle–conditioned Live yeast remains, or may be filtered then re-seeded with fresh yeast	>100 weeks	Yeast in the bottle continues to mature over time, producing more complex flavours and CO_2. If yeast dies, harsh savoury flavours may appear.

"Beer, if drunk in moderation, softens the temper, cheers the spirit and promotes health."
Thomas Jefferson 3rd US President

TORTUOUS JOURNEYS

Between the brewer putting the beer in its package, and you getting it in your glass, several things can influence the flavour of your beer. They include;

TIME: See shelf life

TRANSPORT: Repeated handling in transit to the supermarket or cellar does not pose a problem to brewery-conditioned canned, bottled or kegged beer but it can for cask-conditioned beer. *Cask beer* uses proteins called *finings* to help settle the yeast out of the beer in the pub cellar. They are effective two or three times, however the more a cask is moved, left to settle, then moved again, the chances of reaching perfect clarity in the glass are reduced.

TEMPERATURE: Extremes of temperature can affect all beers, which can be prematurely aged by excess heat, or cycles of heat and cold.

TIPS

When buying check the 'Best Before Dates'. Will it still be fresh when you drink it?

- ☞ Ideally beer should be stored in a cellar or cool, dry and dark place
- ☞ Always drink the oldest beer first

Beer will not harbour any harmful bacteria, and therefore does not have a 'Use By' date. The 'Best Before' date is determined by the brewer as the time within which they will vouch for the products taste quality.

A PINT IN THE PUB

Brewers *sterilise* casks and kegs *before filling* them to ensure the beer is free from microbial contamination with wild yeast, mould or bacteria that may spoil its flavour. Once filled, the container is sealed to preserve that freshness.

To get that beer into your glass, the container has to be 'broached' by the licensee and the *beer passed up a line*, through the tap and into your glass. This simple journey, the last few yards of the beer's route to its final destination, is the most *threatening to beer quality*.

Serving good quality beer, consistently, depends on skilled cellar and barstaff. Staff who understand beer, maintain dispense equipment, have good hygiene standards, control temperatures and ensure beer is not on sale for to long.

"Q"

"The church is near, but the road is icy.
The bar is far away, but I will walk carefully."
Russian proverb

HOW COOL!

Drinking temperature impacts upon your perception of beer flavour and balance, because lower temperatures inhibit aroma evaporation, they also reduce the sensitivity to some taste and mouthfeel elements.
So...

lower temperature = less perceived flavour

higher temperature = more perceived flavour

There are generally accepted or popular drinking temperatures, but ultimately there is no such thing as the correct drinking temperature, it's all down to *personal preference*. For example, you might expect India Pale Ale to be served at cellar temperature, but I also like it chilled with a spicy curry. However, I wouldn't drink an American Light beer anything other than ice cold, as usually recommended.

The popular conventions of drinking temperature are normally cellar temperature or below.
For specifics, see the ALL **BEER** FLAVOUR GUIDE.

TIPS

DRINKING TEMPERATURE

Cask or packaged Ales:
11-13°C
(cellar temperature)

Keg Ales, sparkling or creamflow:
8-10°C

Standard Lager, super-chilled Ales & stouts:
5-7°C

Super-chilled Lager:
0-4°C

Top 3 Beer Head Killers:
Poor glasswashing
Peanuts & fatty snacks
Lipstick

SMELLS LIKE CAT PEE?

The bottle colour isn't just aesthetic, or to make the label stand out. *The glass colour can affect beer flavour*, honestly!

Some hop compounds can be *triggered by light* to create thiols, which create the pungently aromatic characters termed *lightstruck*, 'skunky' or 'cat pee'. These putrid smells, like burning rubber or cat urine, are *1000 times stronger* than other beer aromas.

Clear glass offers no protection, green glass offers some and *brown glass protects* against lightstruck completely. Some beers, like Sol and Miller, use specially treated hop extracts, allowing them to use clear glass without the 'cat pee' problem.

"Let no man thirst for good beer."
Sam Adams US Founding Father

CLASS IN A GLASS

Style statements are all part of the drinking experience however, drinking from the bottle *diminishes the flavour* experience. You could argue that for some beers this is an advantage!

The type of glass your beer is served in will impact on the presentation and beer flavour.

TIPS

GLASSWARE

1. Tall, tapered to the base. Helps preserve the head.

2. Bulbous base and stem. Easy swirling maximises aromas

3. Tapered-in mouth. Funnel effect concentrates aromas

4. Etched ring. 'Nucleation' sites form bubbles

❶ ❷ ❸ ❹

Towel drying glasses is unhygienic, can spoil the taste, kill the head and cause bubble nucleation on the glass sides.

TIPS

GLASSWARE

1. Tapered-out mouth – dissipate aromas from strong beers.
2. Tall glasses, tapered at the rim – pour beer onto the middle & back of the tongue, accentuating sharp and bitter flavours.
3. Straight-brimmed glasses – pour beer over the full length of the tongue, assisting full appreciation of all characters.
4. Low, wide glasses encourage sipping – placing beer on the front of the tongue enhancing fruit and sweet flavours.

❶ ❷ ❸ ❹

MAX THE TASTE

ALL BEER's FLAVOURMAX glass was specially selected to maximise the flavours across the full range of beer styles.

ALL BEER's FLAVOURMAX glass is:

- bowled to allow swirling and release aromas
- nipped-in to chimney those aromas to your nose
- straight-lipped to pour beer over the length of your tongue

Therefore it creates as broad a taste and mouthfeel experience as the beer you're tasting will allow.

TRY IT! Appreciating your beer starts with ABi's 1 to 4. Start experiencing!

FLAVOUR: SENSE IT!

Our senses are basic and primeval survival mechanisms. In the case of food & drink, they help protect us from ingesting harmful things. Over time they have evolved to enable us to experience pleasure or displeasure from eating and drinking.

EXPERIENCE THE FLAVOUR

Sensory impulses are experienced in the eyes, nose & mouth and *interpreted by the brain*. All the sensory inputs gather together and give you a perception of *flavour*. So your conscious appreciation of flavour is not in your mouth, but in your head. These sensory impulses can form such *strong memories* that you can recall some flavours from your childhood right now. Remember the aromas, textures and tastes, along with where you were and how it felt!

Over the next few pages ALL **BEER** INTERECTIVE (AB*i*) gives you the chance to *test your tastebuds* with the games I use when hosting beer flavour events. For maximum sensation when you *smell it, taste it and feel it*, use a partner and a blindfold!

AB*i* will help you identify *feature flavours* and pinpoint what new beer styles you might enjoy.

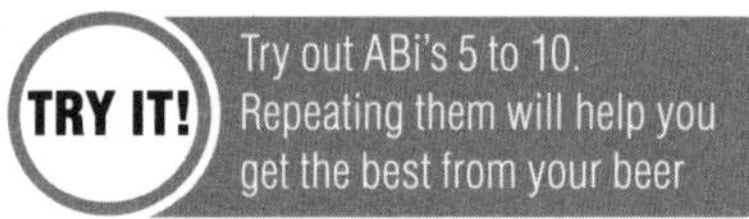

TRY IT!
Try out ABi's 5 to 10.
Repeating them will help you
get the best from your beer

"Q"

"The mouth of a perfectly happy man is filled with beer."
Ancient Egyptian Saying

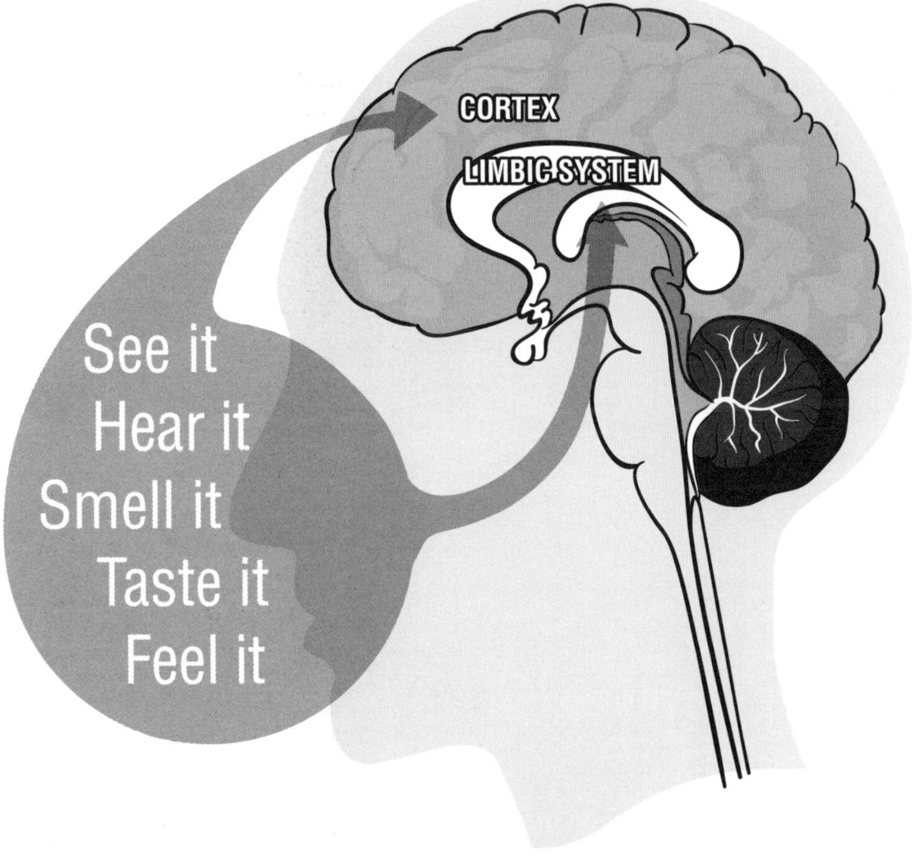

CORTEX

LIMBIC SYSTEM

See it
Hear it
Smell it
Taste it
Feel it

The 'Limbic system' of your brain is crucial to setting your emotional 'tone' and plays a vital role in flavour experience. When excited, it heightens your emotional state and senses. It is intimately linked to forming memories.

SEE IT !

You drink with your eyes first. It's effectively a safety check of whether the beer's presentation meets your expectations. It also starts to set your anticipation of the flavours the beer will have when you drink it.

#5 – SEE IT

There are Four C's for the eyes to take in:

1. **COLOUR**
   from white to gold, amber to black, a fantastic range
2. **CLARITY**
   from cloudy opacity to brilliantly clear and bright
3. **CARBONATION**
   from still and flat to 'Grand Prix' fizz
4. **CLING**
   from clear glass walls to laced drinking rings

What you see around you affects the *way you feel*. Whether it's your living room or garden, local or new bar, in or out of town, beach or mountain, sunshine or snow, your surroundings influence how you feel and your perception of the flavour experience. Different space, different taste!

photo courtesy of The Lamb Inn at Hindon

HEAR IT!

Just as your eyes take in your surroundings, so do your ears. The *buzz* or *calm* around you helps set the mood for your beer experience, whether that's sitting in your favourite seat with the match about to start, or waiting to be served in a bar.

Glugs, whooshes and drips are all sensory parts of liquid refreshment, they heighten your expectation as you imagine your first taste.

Another pleasure principle:
Never let bar staff pour your bottle – you've paid for the privilege, it's all yours.

#6 – HEAR IT

Find an excuse to go and stand at a bar for half an hour.
How many of these sounds can you hear? It's important work!

CLUNK POP KLINK GLUG GLUG GLUG
GURGLE PFSSST CRK'TSSSSSSS
Whssshh Whssshh Whssshh

...the buzz of
a lively bar

...the calm
lapping of waves

SMELL IT!

Aromas are *volatile chemicals* that dissolve in the air. There are a *few thousand unique aromas* that are dissolved, diffused and detected at different rates.

In evolutionary terms, our sense of smell (Olfaction) is one of the most ancient senses. It helps us identify aromas from *food*, mates, predators and provides *sensual pleasure*, as well as warning of some harmful chemicals and organisms.

As we inhale, *aromas* are dissolved in the mucous of the upper nasal cavity and contact the nasal receptor cells that detect each aroma.

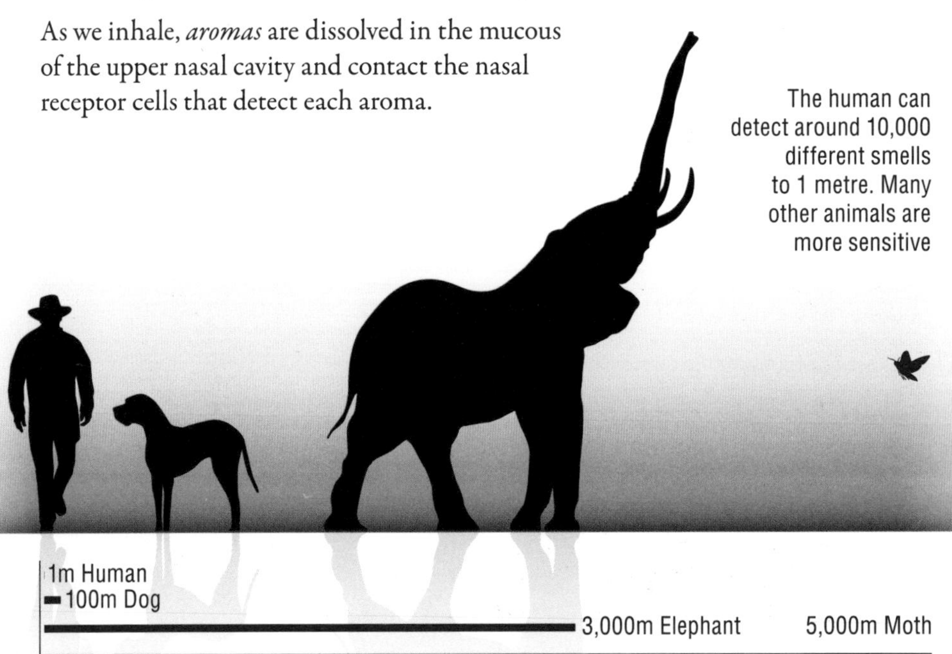
The human can detect around 10,000 different smells to 1 metre. Many other animals are more sensitive
1m Human
100m Dog
3,000m Elephant
5,000m Moth

DATA SOURCE REF#3

AROMA IS THE MAIN DETERMINANT OF FLAVOUR

Experts state that around 80% *of what we perceive as taste, is actually aroma*. For instance, different flavoured artificial soft drinks and jellies are made from similar bases, but they taste dramatically different due to the use of fruit fragrances.

Our memory for aroma lasts a long time, longer than other sensory memories, making them even *more important* in the *flavour* experience. The phenomenon of particular smells evoking memories is known as the 'Proust effect' REF#4

WHO SMELLS THE BEST?

Our *personal ability* to smell varies significantly from one person to another, based upon factors such as gender, sexuality, age, genetic make-up and cultural background. State of health and use of certain drugs can *reduce the ability to smell* too.

Ability to smell *tails off* from your 20's, and by 80 years old 80% of people have some smell dysfunction. *Women* of child-bearing age are thought to have the most acute sense of smell REF#5

Many brewers train this group for their specialist *'taste' panels*. Women's ability to smell continues to out-perform men at all ages.

LOVE IT OR LOATHE IT?

There is huge diversity in beer aroma, ranging from pungently cheesy Lambic beers, to subtly fruity light Lagers. Whether you *love* or *loathe* a particular brand or beer type, is as dependent on your background and cultural experiences as on your genes, age and sex. We all have our own preferences.

#7 – SMELL IT

If you want to train your brain to recognise individual aromas, sniff out these items, whose aromas are commonly found in beer. (See p.168).

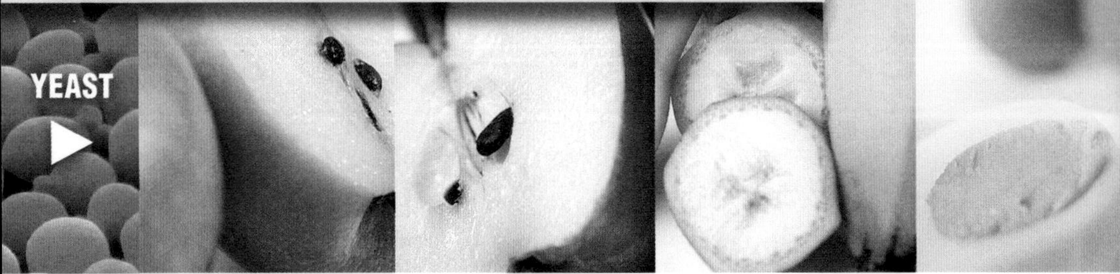

YEAST

MALT

HOPS

Peach

DARK 70%

MEDIUM CUT
ORANGE

TASTE IT!

Taste (Gustation) is one our main 'chemical' senses.
Like smell, it has an evolutionary role in *protecting* the body from ingesting harmful substances and identifying foods that give us *pleasure*.

Chemicals in food and drinks dissolve on the tongue and are detected by around 7000 invisible *taste buds* located on the red dots (taste papillae) on your tongue and around your mouth. These taste buds respond to: bitter, sour, salty, sweet and umami (meaty or savoury) tasting substances.

Most natural toxins and medicines are *bitter* and acids are *sour*. These tastes are often perceived as unpleasant and potentially harmful to the body. *Salty*, *sweet* and *meaty* tastes give us pleasure, signalling they are desirable to the bodies development or maintenance. Balanced combinations of tastes give us the most satisfying flavour experiences.

CULTURED TASTE?

After smell, taste is the next most *important factor* in flavour perception. Once again, genetics, gender, cultural background and experience play a role in taste ability and preference, however *culture* can override genetic pre-disposition.
Like smell, ability to taste declines with age.

SUPERTASTERS

Some of you will experience more intense taste reactions than others. You might be a supertaster. *Supertasters* tend to have a *greater proportion* of taste buds than the majority of the population, and are *more sensitive* to aroma and mouth-feel too. Supertasters find *bitter* tastes are most pronounced.

In taste tests using a bitter substance, it was found that:

25% are 'supertasters'

50% find moderate bitterness and

25% can't taste it at all. REF#6

More women than men are supertasters.

PAPS AND BUDS

FUNGIFORM

FOLIATE

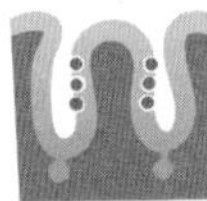

CIRCUMVALLATE

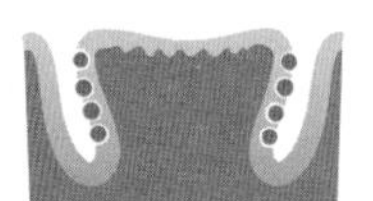

The tongue has 3 kinds of papillae that contain the microscopic taste buds. The numbers of papillae and buds may vary slightly from person to person.

200	Fungiform papillae (button mushroom shaped).	contain about 1120 buds
10	Foliate papillae (around 5 each side, long & thin shaped).	contain about 1280 buds
3 -13	Circumvallate papillae (sunken circular shaped).	contain about 2200 buds
		Tongue total about 4600 buds

Add on another 2500 buds from your epiglottis and other soft palate areas, that makes a total of over 7000 taste buds at work.

Whilst all taste buds are thought to be able to detect all tastes, there does appear to be 'some areas that are more responsive to certain tastes than others' REF#7

As with aroma, people have their own taste sensitivities and preferences. Beer has all the different taste sensations present in quantities that vary with the beer style and brand. Whether you like it sweet, bitter or sour, there's a beer for you.

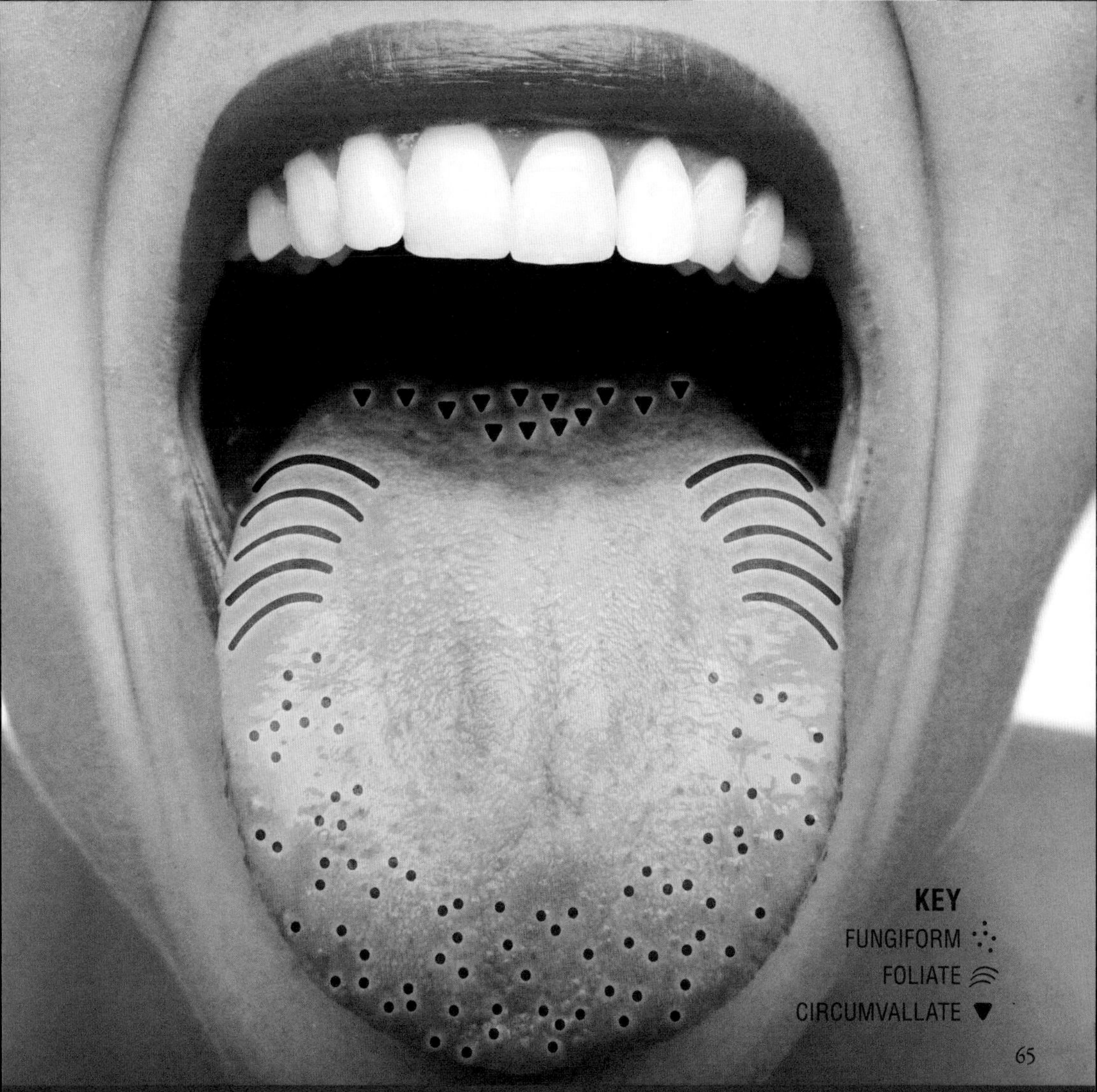

KEY
FUNGIFORM
FOLIATE
CIRCUMVALLATE

#8 – TASTE IT

Try 'Testing your tastebuds' with these common household items.
For maximum effect get a friend to mix the order, close your eyes and HOLD YOUR NOSE so you are not influenced by the sight or aroma. Let each taste sample run across your tongue, is there any part of the tongue where the sensation appears stronger than the others?

SWEET: Dissolve 2 teaspoons of sugar in a mug of boiled water, let it cool. Hold your nose, then take a sip (or use a teaspoon).

SALTY: Dissolve half a teaspoon of table salt in a mug of boiled water, let it cool. Hold your nose, take a sip (or use a teaspoon).

SOUR: Mix 4 teaspoons full of lemon juice in a mug of water. Hold your nose, then take a sip (or use a teaspoon).

BITTER: Pour out a can of tonic water and let it go completely flat. Hold your nose, then take a sip (or use a teaspoon).

UMAMI (SAVOURY): Dissolve half a teaspoon of Bovril, Marmite or beef stock cube in a mug of warm (boiled) water & let it cool. Hold your nose, take a sip (or use a teaspoon).

photo courtesy Andy Fallon www.andyfallon.co.uk

FEEL IT!

Touch and pain receptors are *all over our bodies*, including our eyes, nose and mouth, sending signals to the brain. So, some chemicals in food and drink that we can smell and taste may also be felt. Think pepper.

Feeling includes *touch* and *position, temperature* and *pain*. We become aware of touch first and pain last. When we eat or drink we sense the texture or *mouthfeel* of the food or drink as well as how hot or cold it is.

Mouthfeel is an *important* part of the beer drinking experience, working with taste and aroma to create the *perceived flavour.* Temperature has a critical effect on perceived flavour because *warmer* beers are more volatile with greater aroma, *enhancing* the flavour, while *cooler* beers are less volatile, release fewer aromas and appear more *refreshing.*

TIPS

The main mouthfeel sensations are...

Moisture:
Wetting VS Drying

Temperature:
Warming VS Cooling

Texture:
Smooth VS Astringent

Body (fullness):
Thin VS Full-bodied

Carbonation:
Low VS High

PLEASURE AND PAIN

Temperature perception can be both *physical* (e.g. heat & cold) and *chemical* (e.g. chillies & menthol), and in extremes causes pain. Highly *carbonated beers* cause a mild pain sensation too, amplifying the effect of spicy foods.

Sugars, proteins and fats determine the *texture* and *body* of our food and drink. There are *no fats in beer* so body is influenced by the amounts of *unfermented sugars* and extracts from hop leaves and grain husks.

For alcohol info see
DRINKAWARE.CO.UK

#9 – FEEL IT

Mouthfeel sensations also influence the overall flavour balance of beer.
Test your mouthfeel with these common household items:

TEMPERATURE

Warming VS Cooling:

A sip of vodka VS a menthol mint

BODY/FULLNESS

Thin VS Full bodied:

Sip water VS milk VS cream

TEXTURE

Smooth VS Astringent:

Lick a sliced banana VS Bite into green banana skins.

(Grape pips or sucking a cold wet tea bag, also give the astringent experience).

CARBONATION

None VS High:

Tongue in water VS Tongue in a glass nearly full of cola.

(Other highly-carbonated soft drinks work too). See how long you can hold it there. Try putting it back in. Once you're sensitised it's even more effective!

Drying: No ABi, as tricky to do safely at home.

FLAVOUR COMPOSITION

So, when we refer to '*taste*', we usually mean '*flavour*'. Flavour, is a *total taste sensation*, involving smell, taste and touch sensory information, combined with the perceptions that sight and hearing bring us too.

PERCEIVED FLAVOUR

=

AROMA + TASTE + MOUTHFEEL + SIGHT + HEARING

So, the different senses and their cumulative influence on what we describe as the *flavour* or taste of beer are linked. However, the influence of each sense is variable, dependent upon the particular beer and occasion.

> Our sense of taste, or more accurately *flavour,* is completely personal

As we've found out, perceived *flavour varies* from individual to individual too, based upon a range of variable influences, such as genetics, age, sex, culture, health, drug use and location.

Our senses are fundamental to *laying down memories* and flavour imprints in the brain. They influence our *emotions* and some of our longest lasting memories are of tastes or flavours.

#10 – COMBINED FLAVOURS

Common and pleasurable flavours are a combination of sensations.
The aim here is to be able to recognise what makes up the overall flavour experience.
i.e. which separate aroma, taste and mouthfeel sensations can you identify?

Vodka or Gin & Tonic

Milk and 70% Dark Chocolate

ALCOHOL

Alcohol is a 'hydro-carbon' chemical known as ethanol. At room temperature pure alcohol is a volatile, colourless liquid and it only starts to freeze at -114°C, which means beer can be chilled down to around -2°C before freezing.

Alcohol is produced as a natural by-product of the yeast eating wort sugars during fermentation. The amount of alcohol formed depends largely upon the original sugar concentration in wort, referred to as original gravity (OG) or extract. The amount of alcohol is measured by distilling a fixed volume or weight of beer, i.e. % Alcohol By Volume or ABV.

Most beers have an ABV of between 3.5 – 5.5%. Fermentation tends to stop at around 7% ABV as the alcohol becomes toxic to yeast, so it settles out or dies. Stronger ABV beers start out with a higher OG and are usually pitched with fresh yeast several times to increase the ABV, up to a max. of about 20%.

IMPACT ON FLAVOUR

Alcohol affects the 3 major flavour contributors:

Aroma

Alcohol has its own distinct aroma, quite noticeable at over 5% ABV. Its volatility lifts other aromas, making them more noticeable too. Some yeasts also release more complex alcohols that bring liqueur or wine-like aromas.

Taste

Alcohol has a slightly sweet taste, not surprising, as sugars are hydro-carbons with a similar chemical structure. How sweet it appears will depend on your own taste buds.

Mouthfeel

Alcohol creates a false-heat effect, which gives a pleasant warming sensation. It acts together with sweet, body and smoothness to balance more sour, bitter and astringent characters.

The unique ALL **BEER** FLAVOUR GUIDE gives you an insight into the 25 most popular and specialist beer styles within the Ale, Lager and Lambic families.

It pulls together their background, the building blocks that make their flavours unique and distinctive, alcohol strength range, serving temperatures and an indication of typical attributes of that beer style, i.e. what's in store for your senses if you try them out.

TYPICAL A.B.V.
4.2–6.0%
SERVING TEMPERATURE
11–13°C

style 1

Pale Ale

WHAT IS IT? Classic British Ales, of the style developed in Burton On Trent, England during the 18th and 19th century.

Includes India Pale Ale (IPA), the strongest, most highly-hopped versions, brewed to withstand the long voyage to India and quench the thirsts of the Raj.

BUILDING BLOCKS

WATER	Hard water
MALT	Pale ale, crystal and maybe chocolate
HOPS	Liberal quantities of hops for bitterness & aroma
YEAST	Ale yeast, could be multiple strains. Several are bottle-conditioned
OTHERS	Maybe additional sugar or a little wheat

SENSE IT

SEE IT
Dark gold to amber with a creamy white and long-lasting foam

SMELL IT
Floral and spicy hops; apples and bananas, toffee, nuts, eggs & struck matches

TASTE IT
Biscuity sweetness, slightly sharp and a long bitter finish

FEEL IT
Full bodied and warming, drying and astringent

OVERALL IMPRESSION: Robust beers with a boat-load of aromas, full and rounded, balancing high levels of bitterness and a drying finish.

KEY WORD: Hearty

TYPICAL A.B.V.
3.6–5.0%
SERVING TEMPERATURE
11–13°C

style 2

Bitter

WHAT IS IT? Bitter is an Ale style brewed throughout Britain, traditionally cask-conditioned and easier to drink than Pale Ales. They are termed 'Bitter' to distinguish them from Mild and Brown Ales. 'Best ' Bitters tend to be the brewers mainstay brand while 'Special' Bitters tend to be stronger or with particular ingredients e.g. a distinctive hop variety.

BUILDING BLOCKS

WATER	Medium hard
MALT	Pale Ale, crystal
HOPS	A good helping, may be several varieties
YEAST	Ale yeast, could be multiple strains
OTHERS	Sugar syrup, wheat flour or flaked maize may be used in small proportion

SENSE IT

SEE IT

Range from deep gold to dark nut brown, usually served with a thick, creamy head

SMELL IT

May include floral, spicy and earthy hops, citrus fruits, apples and banana with a range of malt, nut and roast characters

TASTE IT

Salts and malts balancing a bitter finish

FEEL IT

Generally well-balanced with a drying, quenching finish

OVERALL IMPRESSION: Refreshing blends of biscuit and light roasted malts balanced by floral and spicy hops and subtle fruits with a drying, bitter finish.

KEY WORD: Quenching

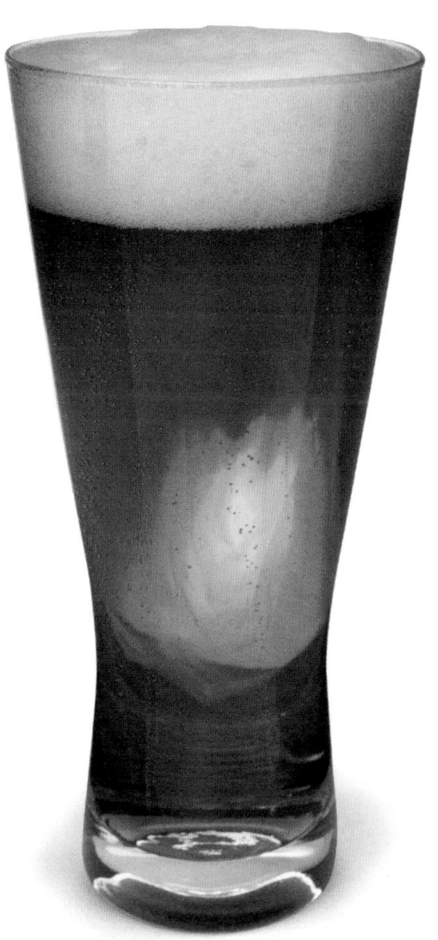

TYPICAL A.B.V.
3.0–5.0%
SERVING TEMPERATURE
6–10°C

style 3

Brown Ale

WHAT IS IT? Primarily a northern British Ale style, developed in the early 20th century with a dark colour and sweeter taste, to separate them from more Bitter and Pale Ales. Similar to the Scotch Ales from north of the Border. Southern English Brown Ales tend to be sweeter with lower ABV. Usually bottled.

BUILDING BLOCKS

WATER	Medium hard
MALT	Pale ale with crystal, caramel & chocolate malts
HOPS	Low levels of bitterness and aroma hop
YEAST	Ale yeast
OTHERS	May use caramel

SENSE IT

SEE IT
Sparkling ales with dark amber to rich ruby and tawny brown body, dark creamy and coffee coloured heads

SMELL IT
Liquorice and treacle toffee, caramel malt, a tad of coffee

TASTE IT
Pretty sweet, minimal bitterness

FEEL IT
Full and rounded, may have a drying finish

OVERALL IMPRESSION: Full-on buttery sweet malt characteristics including toffee and nuts, low fruit and hop contribution.

KEY WORD: Caramel

TYPICAL A.B.V.
3.0–3.9%
SERVING TEMPERATURE
11–13°C

style 4

Mild

WHAT IS IT? Essentially the draught version of Brown Ale, Mild was once the biggest selling beer style. It retains popularity in the industrial heartlands of South Wales, the Midlands and Northwest England.

BUILDING BLOCKS

WATER	Relatively soft
MALT	Pale ale, crystal and roasted
HOPS	Minimal use for subtle character
YEAST	Ale yeast
OTHERS	Maybe roasted wheat, sugar or caramel

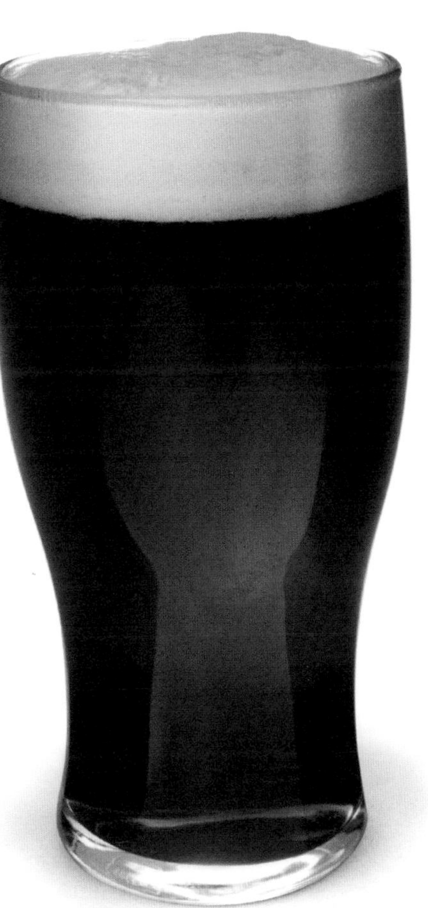

SENSE IT

SEE IT
Ruby, tawny or nearly black with a creamy coffee head

SMELL IT
Subtle hops and fruits with lots of roast malt, caramel, toffee and coffee

TASTE IT
Sweet with minimal bitterness

FEEL IT
Smooth and rounded but not full-bodied

OVERALL IMPRESSION: Usually light in taste and dark in colour, gently hopped and easy to drink, dominated by toasted malt with a little fruit.

KEY WORD: Toasted

TYPICAL A.B.V.
3.5–7.0%
SERVING TEMPERATURE
5–10°C

style 5

Scotch Ale

WHAT IS IT? Scottish Ales, similar in style to Northeast England's Brown Ales, with low hops and a variety of strengths, often termed by the old duty rates such as 'Light' or 60 shilling; 70 shilling 'Heavy' and 80 shilling 'Export' with the strongest , 90 shilling beers termed 'Wee Heavy'.

BUILDING BLOCKS

WATER	Medium soft
MALT	Pale ale, crystal, chocolate and black malts
HOPS	Used sparingly and well-boiled
YEAST	Ale yeast, fermented cool
OTHERS	Roasted barley, malted wheat

SENSE IT

SEE IT
Rich amber and red to dark chestnut brown with a loose creamy coffee-coloured foam

SMELL IT
Malt and fruit dominate with caramel, toffee and chocolate, toasted grains and a wide range of fruit

TASTE IT
Big and sweet, not much bitterness and a touch of acidity

FEEL IT
Full and rounded, often warming but served cool

OVERALL IMPRESSION: Sweet, full bodied and dark, with rich caramelised malt flavours and fruit aroma but little trace of hops.

KEY WORD: Toffee apple

TYPICAL A.B.V.
3.8–5.5%
SERVING TEMPERATURE
6–10°C

style 6

Blonde & Summer Ales

WHAT IS IT? The Ale brewer's most recent answer to Lager. Starting in the US and adopted by UK micro and even large Regional Ale brewers. Very pale Ale with subtle hop and fruit aromas, often served colder than traditional cask and bottled Ales. Sometimes called Golden Ales.

BUILDING BLOCKS

WATER	Medium hard
MALT	Pale pilsner and pale ale malts only
HOPS	Floral and citrussy hops for fragrance and moderate bitterness
YEAST	Ale yeast
OTHERS	Sugar syrup, wheat, maize or honey for low-colour fermentability

SENSE IT

SEE IT
Light straw to gold, with a fine bright white head

SMELL IT
Typically floral and citrus hops with some light fruit and grainy malt

TASTE IT
Biscuity malt sweetness with tangy acidity and gentle bitter finish

FEEL IT
Light to medium bodied with moderate carbonation and smoothness

OVERALL IMPRESSION: Refreshing, easy drinking beers, light in colour and body with fruity aromas and a sweet tangy finish.

KEY WORD: Fruity

TYPICAL A.B.V.
5.0–10.0%
SERVING TEMPERATURE
11–13°C

style 7

Old Ale

WHAT IS IT? Old Ales share similar recipes to Milds but with alcohol strength and flavour dials turned up to 'Max'. They are often aged in tanks or bottles in the brewery. Often termed 'Winter warmers'.

BUILDING BLOCKS

WATER	Medium hard
MALT	Pale ale, crystal & maybe some black malt
HOPS	Enough to give moderate bitterness, sometimes dry-hopped too
YEAST	Ale yeast, re-pitched to give alcohol strength
OTHERS	Brewing sugar, wheat & caramel may be added too

SENSE IT

SEE IT

Rich, thick & dark with a creamy head

SMELL IT

Intense stewed and preserved fruit, peppery hops and strong liqueur alcohol balanced by full, sweet, treacly malt

TASTE IT

A big mouthful, bitter-sweet and maybe a hint of sourness

FEEL IT

Wallop. Full, rounded, warming and smooth with a long lingering finish

OVERALL IMPRESSION: A real Christmas cake of a beer, ripe fruit and sugary malt aromas balanced by moderate bitterness and rich cream sherry warmth.

KEY WORD: Rich

TYPICAL A.B.V.
7.0–12.0%
SERVING TEMPERATURE
14–16°C

style 8

Barley Wine

WHAT IS IT? The 18th century British answer to French wine imports. Ales brewed to Wine strength, traditionally served in small measures and for good reason. They'll blow your socks off!

BUILDING BLOCKS

WATER	Medium hard
MALT	Pale ale, maybe some crystal
HOPS	Just sufficient to balance
YEAST	Ale yeast, re-pitched as necessary
OTHERS	None

SENSE IT

SEE IT
Mid to dark amber body with a creamy head of fine bubbles

SMELL IT
Huge wafts of alcohol liqueur, orchard and vine fruits and spicy hops with thick syrupy malt

TASTE IT
Sweet and fruity with big balancing bitterness

FEEL IT
Warming alcoholic glow, full and chewy with a long drying finish

OVERALL IMPRESSION: BAMM! Intense alcohol and rich fruits, blended with peppery hops and strong sweet malt.

KEY WORD: Intense

TYPICAL A.B.V.
3.0–9.0%
SERVING TEMPS
8–13°C
14–16°C
IMPERIAL

style 9

Porter & Stout

WHAT IS IT? Originating in the 18th century trading ports of London & Dublin, Porter and Stout use very hard water, dark malts and barley and copious hops to create distinctive near-black beers. Some are softened and sweetened with oats or chocolate. Imperial Stouts are the strongest variants, like those historically shipped to the Russian Imperial courts.

BUILDING BLOCKS

WATER	Very hard
MALT	Pale ale, chocolate and black malts
HOPS	Large amounts added, mainly for bitterness
YEAST	Ale yeast
OTHERS	Roasted barley, flaked barley, oats, chocolate, milk lactose, oysters

SENSE IT

SEE IT

Black as night with scarlet-tinged edges and a creamy coffee foam

SMELL IT

Intense roasted malts, liquorice, coffee and chocolate with a smidge of tart fruit

TASTE IT

Porters tend to greater sweetness and Stouts to sour and bitter

FEEL IT

Big and full with smoothness and astringency in equal measure, often warming and drying too

OVERALL IMPRESSION: Espresso dark, intensely roasted, full bodied and full flavoured. Sweet or sour with a long bitter finish.

KEY WORD: Velvet

TYPICAL A.B.V.
4.3–6.0%

SERVING TEMPERATURE
5–10°C

style 10

Kölsch

WHAT IS IT? Straw-coloured Ale, fermented warm, then cold conditioned. Pronounced ker•lsh, it is protected by the 'Kölsch Convention' that limits brewing to the city of Cologne (Köln), which boasts more than 20 breweries. Traditionally gulped from straight-sided 0.1L 'Stößche' glasses.

BUILDING BLOCKS

WATER	Soft
MALT	Pale pilsner, carapils or crystal
HOPS	Only moderate hop addition
YEAST	Ale yeast, warm fermented
OTHERS	Maybe a little wheat malt

SENSE IT

SEE IT
Yellow to gold in colour with an exuberant bright white foam

SMELL IT
Biscuit and bready malts together with orchard fruits and perfumed hops

TASTE IT
Sweetness from grainy malt with moderate bitterness

FEEL IT
Medium-bodied with a creamy smooth mouthfeel and tangy finish

OVERALL IMPRESSION: Visually Lager-like and served chilled, these Ales are dominated by light malt, floral and fruit aromas leaving a soft, dry finish.

KEY WORD: Fragrant

TYPICAL A.B.V.
5.0–9.0%
SERVING TEMPERATURE
5–10°C

style 11

Belges & Speciale Belges

WHAT IS IT? Tipping a nod to their favoured British beer styles, Belgium's brewers produce their own fine Ales with characteristic flair.
Their interpretations and adaptations using imported British and Continental materials have created some of the World's most reputable beers.

BUILDING BLOCKS

WATER	Soft to medium hard
MALT	Pale pilsner and ale, crystal, Vienna
HOPS	Wide range used for bitterness and aroma
YEAST	Multiple Ale yeast strains. Like Trappist beers, may use 'Dubbel', 'Tripel 'or 'Quadrupel' fermentation. Some are bottle conditioned
OTHERS	Sugar

SENSE IT

SEE IT

Range from straw gold to dark amber with high condition and customary large, loose foamy heads

SMELL IT

Intense perfumy aromas of citrus fruit and pears, toasted and nutty grains with liqueur-like alcohol

TASTE IT

Sweet malt and fruits with big tart bitter finish

FEEL IT

Superbly balanced with even body and warmth, great smoothness and crisp finish

OVERALL IMPRESSION: Refined beers with great balance of light toasted malts, fruity yeast, fragrant hop and alcoholic liqueur traits. Often stronger, but more subtle, than British Ales styles.

KEY WORD: Lavish

TYPICAL A.B.V.
5.0–11.0%
SERVING TEMPERATURE
8–13°C

style 12

Trappist & Abbey

WHAT IS IT? Beers brewed by, or in the style of, the traditional brewer Monks of Belgium and Holland. There are 7 original and protected 'Trappist' beers. Initially created without commercial motivation.

Abbey beers don't always carry the same heritage and may be owned or brewed by larger, more commercial brewers. Both styles carry big distinctive flavours.

BUILDING BLOCKS

WATER	Medium hard
MALT	Pale pilsner and ale, Munich, crystal, carapils
HOPS	Varied use dependent upon brewery and strength
YEAST	Historic Ale yeast cultures and multiple warm fermentations 'Dubbel ' (twice), 'Tripel' (three times) or 'Quadrupel' (four times fermented). Final fermentation in bottle
OTHERS	White or brown sugar

SENSE IT

SEE IT

Bottle-conditioning means complete clarity is not guaranteed. Colours range from gold through amber and red to russet brown, all with lively foam

SMELL IT

Ripe and preserved fruits, rich malts with chocolate and coffee, spicy and floral hops and alcoholic liqueur

TASTE IT

Range from full and sweet to sour and bitter but generally well balanced

FEEL IT

Generally very smooth, stronger versions exude warmth and range from full-bodied to bone dry with high carbonation

OVERALL IMPRESSION: Guaranteed to be strong and full-flavoured, though no unifying style exists. The authentic Trappist appellation mark identifies the originals.

KEY WORD: Elaborate

TYPICAL A.B.V.
4.0–7.0%
SERVING TEMPERATURE
11–13°C

style 13

Bier de Garde & Saison

WHAT IS IT? Pale Ales brewed in the Flanders area of Northern France and in Belgium during Autumn and Winter and stored for Summer drinking (de Garde) or for drinking fresh (Saison). Traditionally served to farm labourers in the field as 'liquid bread'.

BUILDING BLOCKS

WATER	Soft
MALT	Pale ale, crystal, caramel, Munich, carapils & chocolate
HOPS	Range of continental hops, used sparingly
YEAST	Ale and Lager yeasts may be used, warm fermented
OTHERS	Brewing sugar, honey

SENSE IT

SEE IT

Range from straw gold to pale amber and copper-coloured with fine, well conditioned, heads of foam

SMELL IT

Full on biscuit and caramel malts, with sherry-like scents of citrus and grapes, and subtle floral and peppery hops

TASTE IT

Sweet with moderate bitterness and slight acidity

FEEL IT

Quite full bodied and warming with high levels of soft carbonation and a smooth finish

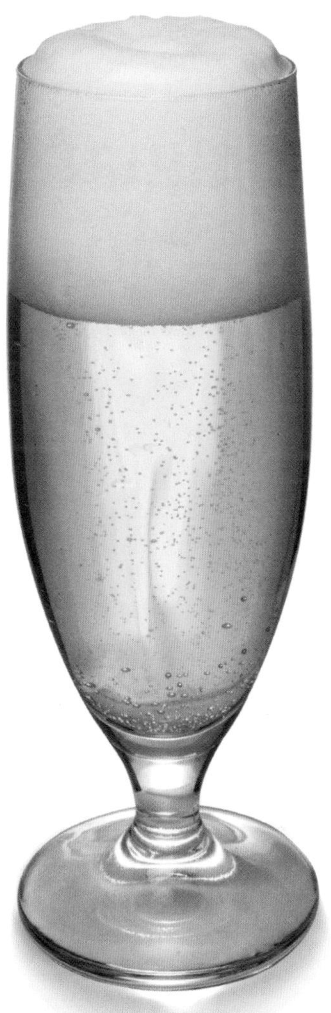

OVERALL IMPRESSION: Full-flavoured but quite refreshing, dominated by biscuity malts and lots of fresh and vinous fruits.

KEY WORD: Biscuity

TYPICAL A.B.V.
4.5–8.0%
SERVING TEMPERATURE
5–14°C

style 14

Belgian Brown & Fruit Ales

WHAT IS IT? Old Brown or 'Oud Bruin' beers are Flemish brown Ales traditionally brewed, like Saison and Biere de Garde, as 'liquid bread' provisions for local farm workers.

'Framboises' versions have raspberries and 'Krieks' have cherries added for a second fermentation, delivering distinctive fruit flavours. These are distinct in flavour from similarly named Lambic fruit beers – always check the labels.

BUILDING BLOCKS

WATER	Medium hard
MALT	Pale ale, Munich, carapils, Vienna red, chocolate,
HOPS	For moderate bitterness only
YEAST	Ale yeast. Some are bottle conditioned
OTHERS	Sugar, roasted barley

SENSE IT

SEE IT
Ruby red to tawny brown, often opaque due to unfiltered yeast, forms a loose head and a reddish tinge

SMELL IT
Intense berry fruits and acid sharpness, offset by rich dark, chocolaty malts

TASTE IT
Sharp at first but sweetens with a hint of peppery bitterness

FEEL IT
Medium bodied with some warmth and a slightly dry bitter finish

OVERALL IMPRESSION: These are fruity Ales, even before any fruit is added. Rich malts and often a touch of acidity. Peppery bitterness and chocolate blend well with the hallmark flavours of intense berries.

KEY WORD: Luscious

TYPICAL A.B.V.
4.3–5.5%
SERVING TEMPERATURE
5–7°C

style 15

Wheat Beers

WHAT IS IT? Ales brewed with minimum 30% wheat.

Germans and Belgian's have brewed beers using wheat for centuries. German styles, termed 'Weisse' (white) or 'Weizen' (wheat) tend to use cereals only, whereas Belgian 'Witte' (white) styles use orange curaçao and herbs such as coriander to flavour.

Berliner Weisse is purposely soured using Lactic acid bacteria.

BUILDING BLOCKS

WATER	Soft
MALT	Pale pilsner, wheat, Vienna and dark malts
HOPS	Low level hops addition for subtle aroma and preservative qualities
YEAST	Ale yeast. Some condition with Lager yeast or Lactic bacteria
OTHERS	Orange peel, coriander, rye, spelt

SENSE IT

SEE IT

Range from very pale white-yellow to rich bronze and even dark brown, mostly unfiltered and cloudy with yeast and wheat protein

SMELL IT

Big fruit fragrances of bananas, apples and citrus with bubblegum and a 'hint of phenolic disinfectant' (may be recognised as medicinal), spicy cloves and smoky malts

TASTE IT

Range from mild to very tart sourness, with biscuity sweet balance and the subtlest of bitter finishes

FEEL IT

Well carbonated but exceedingly smooth mouthfeel with little astringency

OVERALL IMPRESSION: Refreshingly light and well-balanced with soft carbonation and big fruity aromas, a hint of sourness and varying levels of 'medicinal' character.

KEY WORD: Aromatic

TYPICAL A.B.V.
4.4–5.5%

SERVING TEMPERATURE
6–10°C

style 16

Czech Pilsner

WHAT IS IT? The original pale Lager style. The brand Pilsner Urquell, literally translates from Czech as 'the original from Plzen'. Created in 1842, this was the first truly pale beer.

This authentic Pilsner Lager style is used throughout the breweries of the Czech Republic, producing full-flavoured beers, often Lagered for as long as 3 months. It is the style from which all other pale Lagers are derived.

BUILDING BLOCKS

WATER	Very soft
MALT	Moravian pilsner malt
HOPS	Substantial Saaz hop addition for bitterness and late-hop for aroma
YEAST	Lager yeast
OTHERS	May use brewing sugar

SENSE IT

SEE IT

Straw gold to pale amber beer served with a full and fine white head

SMELL IT

Spicy and herbal hops overlay rich buttery and biscuity malts with subtle fruit mixed in for good measure. Hints of lemongrass, wood, bubblegum and maybe a bit of butterscotch

TASTE IT

Biscuity malt sweetness perfectly balanced by lengthy but not aggressive bitterness

FEEL IT

Softly carbonated and silky smooth delivery, rounded and warming with moderate astringency to finish

OVERALL IMPRESSION: Smooth, full-bodied and full-flavoured. Superbly well balanced between biscuity malts, herbal hops and fruity yeast flavours.

KEY WORD: Seasoned

TYPICAL A.B.V.
5.0–6.0%
SERVING TEMPERATURE
5–7°C

style 17

Continental Pilsener

WHAT IS IT? German and wider European interpretations of the Czech Pilsner style. Influenced by German Pils beers, which are usually more fully fermented than Czech Pilsners, and consequently have less body and a more drying finish.

Some beers still adhere to the German Reinheitsgebot of 1516, while other Continental brewers create flavour distinction using sugars or other grains.

BUILDING BLOCKS

WATER	Soft
MALT	Pale pilsner
HOPS	Significant hop addition for bitterness, possible late hop for aroma
YEAST	Lager yeast, cold fermented
OTHERS	Brewing sugar, wheat, maize

SENSE IT

SEE IT
Range from yellow to pale gold, crystal clear with an enduring white head

SMELL IT
Light grainy malt and floral hops often with hints of cooked vegetable, sweetcorn or baked bean character

TASTE IT
Some acidity, a little grainy sweetness and a bitter finish

FEEL IT
Quite highly carbonated with a clean mouthfeel and dry finish

OVERALL IMPRESSION: Crisper and more refreshing than Czech Pilsners, often less aromatic, with a more bitter drying finish.

KEY WORD: Crisp

TYPICAL A.B.V.
4.5–6.0%
SERVING TEMPERATURE
8–10°C

style 18

Amber, Märzen & Oktoberfest

WHAT IS IT? Influenced by Vienna-style Amber Lager, Bavarian brewers used Vienna malts within the last 'Märzen' beers of the brewing season in March. The beer was stored in ice-caves over summer and broached after the harvest at the Autumn 'Oktoberfest'.

Austrian migrants took the Amber Lager style to Mexico.

BUILDING BLOCKS

WATER	Medium hard
MALT	Pale pilsner, Munich, Vienna and crystal malts
HOPS	Hop addition for moderate bitterness and aroma
YEAST	Lager yeast and cold fermentation
OTHERS	Sugar syrup, maize

SENSE IT

SEE IT

Bright beer with a warm orange amber to deep copper glow and off-white foam

SMELL IT

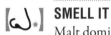

Malt dominated, with fresh bread or biscuity malt and hints of toffee, nuts, coffee and chocolate. Low fruit and little hop aroma

TASTE IT

Well-balanced dark malt sweetness with moderate bitterness

FEEL IT

Nice body, very smooth and softly carbonated with a slightly dry finish

OVERALL IMPRESSION: Characterful, smooth beers with a range of rich malt flavours. Influenced by easy-drinking American beers, Mexican Amber Lagers are less full-bodied and flavoured.

KEY WORD: Konditorei

TYPICAL A.B.V.
4.0–5.0%
SERVING TEMPERATURE
0–7°C

style 19

Helles Pale Lagers

WHAT IS IT? Originally a pale Lager style in it's own right, created by Bavarian brewers and called 'Hell' (meaning light) to distinguish it from their dark beers.

Many popular Lagers now fit into this category. Whilst German Helles beers tend to adhere to the Reinheitsgebot, pale Lagers from elsewhere in the World may use a wide variety of other fermentable starch sources.

BUILDING BLOCKS

WATER	Soft or very soft
MALT	Pale pilsner
HOPS	Moderate addition for bitterness and aroma
YEAST	Lager yeast, cold fermented
OTHERS	Sugar syrup, wheat, maize, rice, soarghum

SENSE IT

SEE IT
Light yellow to pale gold, clear and bright with tight white foam

SMELL IT
Very subtle hops and grainy malt with light fruit and maybe some vegetable aroma

TASTE IT
Sweetish, grainy malt tends to moderate bitterness. Balanced

FEEL IT
Moderate body, carbonation smoothness and astringency with no extremes

OVERALL IMPRESSION: The Helles style covers many of the biggest-selling beers in the World delivering clean tasting, refreshing, drinkable beers.

KEY WORD: Refreshing

TYPICAL A.B.V.
6.4–14.0%
SERVING TEMPERATURE
11–16°C

style 20

Bock

WHAT IS IT? The Goat beer! Originally brewed in Einbeck, Northern Germany. Bocks are strong Lager beers brewed to celebrate festivals.

The Bavarians adopted the style and evolved the name to 'Bock', the nickname for billy-goat. Many Bock's carry a goat on the label, an emblem of strength and virility. High alcohol variants are termed 'Doppelbock'.

BUILDING BLOCKS

WATER	Medium soft
MALT	Pale pilsner, carapils, Munich, Vienna
HOPS	Moderate hop addition for bitterness
YEAST	Lager yeast, cold fermented over a long period
OTHERS	Sugar syrup

SENSE IT

SEE IT

Golden amber to deep copper and brown. All but Weissbock's are clear and bright. Long-lasting off-white head

SMELL IT

Rich and complex malts dominate with caramel, toasty and chocolate notes. Tangy hops and a range of preserved fruits

TASTE IT

Malt and fruit sweetness dominates the long flavour, with medium bitterness

FEEL IT

Medium to full bodied with moderate carbonation and a warming glow

OVERALL IMPRESSION: Imagine a big-flavoured Lager, on steroids, that's a Bock. Big rich malts, spicy hops and alcohol, complex fruits and chocolate. A huge mouthful.

KEY WORD: Colossal

TYPICAL A.B.V.
4.3–5.0%
SERVING TEMPERATURE
0–4°C

style 21

American & Light Lagers

WHAT IS IT? Refinement of the Helles Lager style to produce beers with low flavour impact, for maximum refreshment and easy drinking, particularly in warmer climates.

North American brewers and migrants have transported the style to Central and South America and the Far East, where light tasting beers are produced using local materials to supplement expensive imported Barley malt.

BUILDING BLOCKS

WATER	Soft or very soft
MALT	Pale pilsner
HOPS	Very low addition
YEAST	Lager yeast, cold fermented
OTHERS	Sugar syrup, wheat, maize, rice

SENSE IT

SEE IT
Bright beer of very pale white/ yellow to medium straw colour with sparkling white head that disappears rapidly

SMELL IT
Hop and malt characteristics are subtle or absent. Sugary and yeast-derived fruit or sulphury aromas prevail

TASTE IT
Low level bitterness. Hint of sour may balance any sweetness

FEEL IT
High carbonation bite. Smooth rather than astringent or drying

OVERALL IMPRESSION: The ultimate light-flavoured and easy-drinking beers, served very cold for maximum refreshment.

KEY WORD: Clean

TYPICAL A.B.V.
4.5–6.0%
SERVING TEMPERATURE
5–10°C

style 22

Dunkel & Dark Lager

WHAT IS IT? The way all Lager was before Urquell revolutionised brewing at Plzen. Some Czech and German brewers still brew versions of the dark beers that pre-dated pale Pilsners. Cold fermentation with Lager yeasts ensure that, despite their colour, they remain part of the Lager family.

BUILDING BLOCKS

WATER	Medium soft
MALT	Pale pilsner, dark Munich, dark malt, roasted malt
HOPS	Enough for low to moderate bitterness
YEAST	Lager yeast, cold fermented
OTHERS	Roasted barley

SENSE IT

SEE IT
Deep ruby red to near black in colour with large butter or latte-coloured foam heads

SMELL IT
Rich roasted malt traits dominate with toasted bread, chocolate, nuts and toffee, subtle hops caramel and hints of fruit too

TASTE IT
Surprisingly clean tasting with chocolate malt sweetness tailing off to mild hop & roast bitterness

FEEL IT
Moderate carbonation and body, smooth with a touch of roast malt astringency

OVERALL IMPRESSION: "It's Lager Jim, but not as we know it!" Dark colours belie surprisingly smooth and clean beer, with roast character, gentle bitter-sweet balance and a light dry finish.

KEY WORD: Deceptive

TYPICAL A.B.V.
5.0–6.5%
SERVING TEMPERATURE
11–13°C

style 23

Pure Lambic

WHAT IS IT? An ancient style of beer which allows a natural fermentation with uncultured 'wild' yeasts and other unique atmospheric flora found in Belgium's Senne valley, home to most Lambic brewers. Matured for a year or more to produce characteristic strong flavours.

BUILDING BLOCKS

WATER	Medium soft
MALT	Pilsner malt
HOPS	Aged hops for preservative properties only
YEAST	Natural wild yeast (and bacteria)
OTHERS	At least 30% unmalted wheat

SENSE IT

SEE IT

Pale straw to amber. Cloudiness decreases with age, as does carbonation and head retention

SMELL IT

Decidedly sour and pungent, but softens with maturity as earthy, horsey aromas take over. Oak, citrus, apple, rhubarb and honey aromas may soften the blow!

TASTE IT

No bitterness. Less sour and more sweet malt balanced with age

FEEL IT

Light bodied but full flavoured, low astringency but tart and more drying with age. Very low carbonation

OVERALL IMPRESSION: Naturally cloudy with relatively little head and CO_2 'condition' they are not the most visually appealing beers. Often sour and pungent when young but mellowing with age.

KEY WORD: Pungent

TYPICAL A.B.V.
5.0–8.0%
SERVING TEMPERATURE
8–10°C

style 24

Gueuze

WHAT IS IT? A blend of young and old Lambics to create a more lively carbonated beer. Easier to drink than pure Lambics, Gueuze (pronounced Ger•zer) first appeared in the 19th Century as the Lambic brewers alternative to the rise in popularity of Ales and Lagers.

BUILDING BLOCKS

WATER	Medium soft
MALT	Pilsner malt
HOPS	Aged hops for preservative properties only
YEAST	Natural wild yeast (and bacteria)
OTHERS	At least 30% unmalted wheat

SENSE IT

SEE IT
Highly effervescent, forming a large moussey head over a partially clear (semi-opaque) golden body

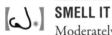

SMELL IT
Moderately sour/acid with farmyard type characters and some fruits, honey, oak and vanilla

TASTE IT
Predominantly sour-sweet, a hint of bitterness may be discernable

FEEL IT
Medium to light-bodied with high carbonation and soft acid/dry finish

OVERALL IMPRESSION: Lambic light! Similar character to the pure Lambic's but with greater CO_2 'condition' and more sweetness balancing sour acidity.

KEY WORD: Zingy

TYPICAL A.B.V.
4.0–5.0%
SERVING TEMPERATURE
8–10°C

style 25

Faro & Lambic Fruit Beers

WHAT IS IT? These beers are typically made with Gueuze rather than pure Lambic and have sugar or fruit added.

Faro has brown sugar added to soften and sweeten the Gueuze.

Lambic Fruit Beers may use a wide variety of fruits to provide sugars and bring in their own unique flavour contributions to a secondary fermentation, often in wooden casks. Fruits used include: cherries (Kriek), raspberries (Framboise), blackcurrants (Cassis), peaches (Peche) and even bananas.

BUILDING BLOCKS

WATER	Medium soft
MALT	Pilsner malt
HOPS	Aged hops for preservative properties only
YEAST	Natural wild yeast (and bacteria)
OTHERS	Unmalted wheat, fruits, brown sugar, sweeteners

SENSE IT

SEE IT

Cloudy. Colour is largely determined by the fruit or sugar used. Fermentation of fruit sugars creates zingy carbonation and a full head, also coloured according to the fruit

SMELL IT

Usual Gueuze characters of sour acid and barnyard aroma's with fruit, honey and oak are suppressed by the added fruit character

TASTE IT

More fruit-led sweetness to balance the tart acidity. No significant bitterness

FEEL IT

Smooth, medium-light body, high carbonation and an increasingly dry finish

OVERALL IMPRESSION: Tart acidity is finely balanced with malt and sweet fruit aromas to create some very smooth, drinkable beers, even for the non beer-drinker. The fruit flavours or sugar molasses introduced soften the traditional Gueuze flavour traits.

KEY WORD: Tangy

HOW TO JUDGE A BEER

The following section will give a simple step by step guide of how to judge a beer. Building on *skills* you developed in the AB*i* sections 1-10. You will be starting to tell your straw's from your ambers, your sours from your astringents and your fruits from your florals.

HOW TO JUDGE A BEER

The following section will give a simple step by step guide of how to judge a beer. Building on *skills* you developed in the **AB*i*** sections 1-10. You will be starting to tell your straw's from your ambers, your sours from your astringents and your fruits from your florals.

The ALL **BEER** FLAVOUR REFERENCE CARDS (FRC's) and *notepad*, are unique templates that have been created to allow you to:

- *Recognise* the distinguishing flavours of common beer styles
- Identify your own *flavour preferences*
- Select *new beer styles* to suit those preferences.
- *Checkout* your skills against the ALL **BEER** GUIDE experts
- Assess other beer styles for yourself

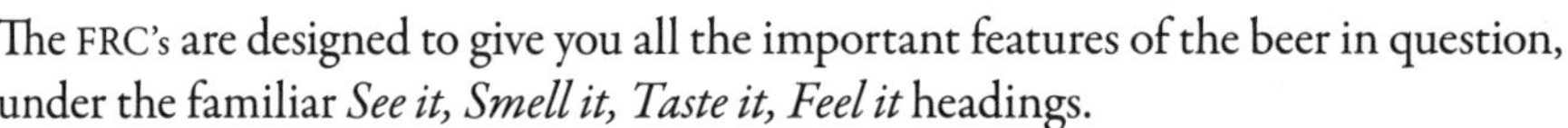

The FRC's are designed to give you all the important features of the beer in question, under the familiar *See it, Smell it, Taste it, Feel it* headings.

The starter set of FRC's included in this guide, are for six well-known beers, to get you familiar with the characteristics of the different styles. Whether you have tasted them before, or not, use them to get a feeling for the 0-5 scales by filling out the flavour notepad and comparing your scores with ours.

For more FRC's, features and information see our website at www.allbeer.co.uk

"Indecision regarding the choice among pleasures temporarily robs a man of inner peace. After due reflection, he attains joy by turning away from the lower pleasures and seeking the higher ones."
I Ching Chinese scripture

ALL BEER FLAVOUR REFERENCE CARDS (FRC's)

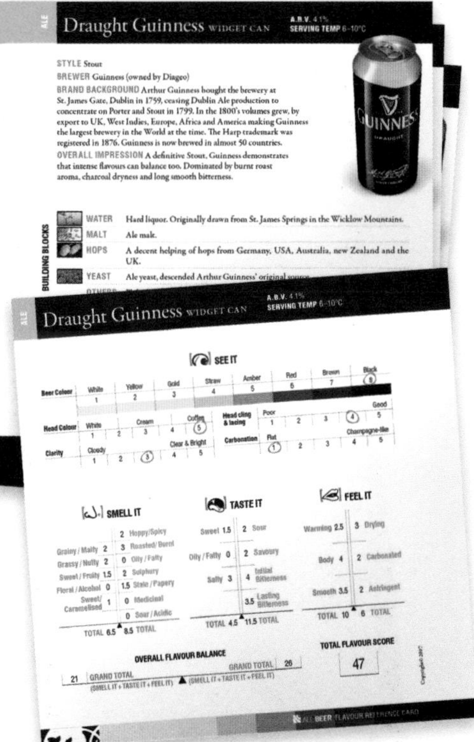

ALE — Draught Guinness WIDGET CAN
A.B.V. 4.1%
SERVING TEMP 6–10°C

STYLE Stout
BREWER Guinness (owned by Diageo)
BRAND BACKGROUND Arthur Guinness bought the brewery at St. James Gate, Dublin in 1759, ceasing Dublin Ale production to concentrate on Porter and Stout in 1799. In the 1800's volumes grew, by export to UK, West Indies, Europe, Africa and America making Guinness the largest brewery in the World at the time. The Harp trademark was registered in 1876. Guinness is now brewed in almost 50 countries.
OVERALL IMPRESSION A definitive Stout, Guinness demonstrates that intense flavours can balance too. Dominated by burnt roast aroma, charcoal dryness and long smooth bitterness.

BUILDING BLOCKS
WATER Hard liquor. Originally drawn from St. James Springs in the Wicklow Mountains.
MALT Ale malt.
HOPS A decent helping of hops from Germany, USA, Australia, new Zealand and the UK.
YEAST Ale yeast, descended Arthur Guinness' original source

ALE — Draught Guinness WIDGET CAN
A.B.V. 4.1%
SERVING TEMP 6–10°C

SEE IT
Beer Colour: White 1, Yellow 2, Gold 3, Straw 4, Amber 5, Red 6, Brown 7, Black (8)
Head Colour: White 1, 2, Cream 3, 4, Coffee (5)
Head cling & lacing: Poor 1, 2, 3, (4), Good 5
Clarity: Cloudy 1, 2, (3), 4, Clear & Bright 5
Carbonation: Flat (1), 2, 3, 4, Champagne-like 5

SMELL IT
Grainy / Malty 2 | 2 Hoppy/Spicy
Grassy / Nutty 2 | 3 Roasted/ Burnt
Sweet / Fruity 1.5 | 0 Oily / Fatty
Floral / Alcohol 0 | 2 Sulphury
Sweet/ Caramelised 1 | 1.5 Stale / Papery
| 0 Medicinal
| 0 Sour / Acidic
TOTAL 6.5 | 8.5 TOTAL

TASTE IT
Sweet 1.5 | 2 Sour
Oily / Fatty 0 | 2 Savoury
Salty 3 | 4 Initial Bitterness
| 3.5 Lasting Bitterness
TOTAL 4.5 | 11.5 TOTAL

FEEL IT
Warming 2.5 | 3 Drying
Body 4 | 2 Carbonated
Smooth 3.5 | 2 Astringent
TOTAL 10 | 6 TOTAL

OVERALL FLAVOUR BALANCE
21 GRAND TOTAL (SMELL IT + TASTE IT + FEEL IT) | GRAND TOTAL 26 (SMELL IT + TASTE IT + FEEL IT)

TOTAL FLAVOUR SCORE
47

ALL BEER FLAVOUR REFERENCE CARD

ALL BEER NOTEPAD

Chart your own experience's to understand and develop your own beer preferences

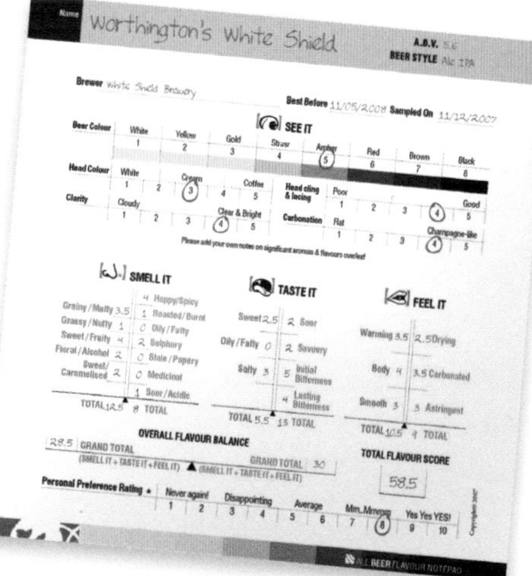

Name Worthington's White Shield
A.B.V. 5.6
BEER STYLE Ale IPA
Brewer White Shield Brewery
Best Before 11/05/2008 Sampled On 11/12/2007

SEE IT
Beer Colour: White 1, Yellow 2, Gold 3, Straw 4, Amber (5), Red 6, Brown 7, Black 8
Head Colour: White 1, 2, Cream (3), 4, Coffee 5
Head cling & lacing: Poor 1, 2, 3, (4), Good 5
Clarity: Cloudy 1, 2, 3, (4), Clear & Bright 5
Carbonation: Flat 1, 2, 3, (4), Champagne-like 5

Please add your own notes on significant aromas & flavours overleaf

SMELL IT
Grainy / Malty 3.5 | 4 Hoppy/Spicy
Grassy / Nutty 1 | 1 Roasted/ Burnt
Sweet / Fruity 4 | 0 Oily / Fatty
Floral / Alcohol 2 | 2 Sulphury
Sweet/ Caramelised 2 | 0 Stale / Papery
| 0 Medicinal
| 1 Sour / Acidic
TOTAL 12.5 | 8 TOTAL

TASTE IT
Sweet 2.5 | 2 Sour
Oily / Fatty 0 | 2 Savoury
Salty 3 | 5 Initial Bitterness
| 4 Lasting Bitterness
TOTAL 5.5 | 13 TOTAL

FEEL IT
Warming 3.5 | 2.5 Drying
Body 4 | 3.5 Carbonated
Smooth 3 | 3 Astringent
TOTAL 10.5 | 9 TOTAL

OVERALL FLAVOUR BALANCE
28.5 GRAND TOTAL (SMELL IT + TASTE IT + FEEL IT) | GRAND TOTAL 30 (SMELL IT + TASTE IT + FEEL IT)

TOTAL FLAVOUR SCORE
58.5

Personal Preference Rating: Never again! 1, 2; Disappointing 3, 4; Average 5, 6; Mm..Mmmm 7, (8); Yes Yes YES! 9, 10

ALL BEER FLAVOUR NOTEPAD

A Zythophile is a lover of beer, from the Greek words Zythos (pronounced ZEE-thos), for beer and Philos, for loving or fond of.

SAVOUR THE FLAVOUR

In this chapter, you have the opportunity to gauge the *flavour* sensations of the beers on the FRC's for yourself, using the *flavour notepad*, and compare your scores with the ALL **BEER** GUIDE experts.

This will help develop your flavour recognition skills, so they become part and parcel of *enjoying your beer*, savouring every flavour. It may also influence your beer choice and *value* judgement in future.

TIPS

TASTING

1. Get your beer at the right temperature
2. Clean/dishwasher & drip-dry your ALL **BEER** FLAVOURMAX™ glass
3. Use a bright room with no other strong aromas,
4. Have the ALL **BEER** FLAVOUR NOTEPAD and pencil ready

"I think this would be a good time for a beer"
President Franklin D. Roosevelt
on signing the repeal of Prohibition

SEE IT, HEAR IT

1. Check out the beer pack for product details such as the brewer, best before date, %ABV etc.
2. POP/PFSSST/CRK-TSSSSssss – open your beer.
3. Take your first sniff from the open pack. Some beers have initial smells that are highly volatile and *disappear* soon after pouring. For example Budweiser has a drainy, sulphury aroma at first, which disappears within minutes leaving a sugary, fruity aroma a bit like candyfloss.
4. Pour some beer into the ALL BEER FLAVOURMAX™ glass. Let a head form by tilting the glass to 45° and pouring from a height of about 100mm (4 inches), straightening the glass as you pour.
5. About 150ml (5fl oz) *is enough* for now, to the widest point of the glass, just below the embossed logo.

4

5

Legal draught beer measures in the UK are ***⅓ Pint, ½ Pint*** *and* ***One Pint,*** *in lined and stamped glasses*

REMEMBER THE 4 C'S?

Visual assessments are rated on a 1 to 5 scale, or 1 to 8 for colour.

SEE IT

Beer Colour	White	Yellow	Gold	Straw	Amber	Red	Brown	Black
	1	2	3	4	5	6	7	8

COLOUR gives you great initial insight into the beer.

- Where about does it appear on the color spectrum?
- Have any darker malts been used, what flavours might you expect?
- Rate the head colour too, this varies a lot for amber or darker beers.

CARBONATION refers to the amount of CO_2 dissolved in the beer. It can't be measured visually, though you can get a good idea.

- Is it *gushing* like Champagne or *still* as a millpond?
- A rising *stream of bubbles* is appealing in highly carbonated beers. You can anticipate a sharp *tingle on your tongue* as you taste it.
- Bubbles carry more aromas to the surface and support the head.

Nitrogen bubbles are far *smaller than* CO_2 bubbles. Think of the millions of miniature swirling bubbles in Guinness or 'creamflow' beers.

"Beauty lies in the hand of the beer-holder"
Sign at California and Front St. San Francisco

CLING or lacing, is when the bubbles in the beer head cling to the glass.

- Malt glycoproteins form the surface of the bubbles, and create the *creamy head* on beer.
- The bubbles are *reinforced* by sticky *hop compounds*, causing the head to last longer and stick to the glass.
- Beers with more hops tend to form a thicker and *longer-lasting* head.
- The head forms *drinking rings* as the glass is emptied.

CLARITY can indicate if beer is aged or infected.

- Only Wheat and Lambic beers should be cloudy.
- All other beers should be clear, bright and appealing (even cask).

Hand-pulled cask beer draws in nitrogen from the air to form a rich creamy head. Widget cans and bottles squirt nitrogen into the beer upon opening to re-create the cask experience at home.

SENSATIONAL SYMMETRY: **Why the Scales?**

Most highly regarded and popular beers, of whatever style, have one thing in common. They are *well-balanced*. Creating a balanced beer is part of the brewer's art. Good balance can be achieved in many different ways, as aroma, taste and mouthfeel all play their part, and differ from beer to beer.

You will notice that we divide *See it, Taste it* and *Feel it* characters into those which are MORE POSITIVE = COPPER and those which are MORE NEGATIVE = GREEN. This is subjective but it allows a balance to be created. It's also important to note that having too many of the more 'positive' characters will unbalance a beer, just as much as an excess of 'negatives'.

Perception of balance is as personal as our own 'sense of taste'. It varies from person to person, however we tend to prefer beers that seem well balanced to us. By comparing tasting notes for the same beer with others, you will learn about how you perceive balance within your own *flavour space*. Remember *fatty* and *savoury* characters play little or no part in good fresh tasting beers.

SMELL IT

		4	Hoppy/Spicy
Grainy / Malty	3.5	1	Roasted/ Burnt
Grassy / Nutty	1	0	Oily / Fatty
Sweet / Fruity	4	2	Sulphury
Floral / Alcohol	2	0	Stale / Papery
Sweet/ Caramelised	2	0	Medicinal
		1	Sour / Acidic
TOTAL	12.5	8	TOTAL

TASTE IT

Sweet	2.5	2	Sour
Oily / Fatty	0	2	Savoury
Salty	3	5	Initial Bitterness
		4	Lasting Bitterness
TOTAL	5.5	13	TOTAL

FEEL IT

Warming	3.5	2.5	Drying
Body	4	3.5	Carbonated
Smooth	3	3	Astringent
TOTAL	10.5	9	TOTAL

"Q" *"Beer... a high and mighty liquor"*
Julius Caesar

SMELL IT: Beeromatherapy

Time to put our most acute sense to the test. We have *two chances* to assess the beer aroma, firstly *through the nose*, by sniffing, then later-on, through *retro-nasal* when tasting. Because the mouth and nose are linked, you release more of the heavier aromas up into your nose via your mouth as you taste.

Here's a chance to improve your *technique*. You'll get more out of it if you go about it in the right way. Beer is less alcoholic than drinks like wine, the aromas are often *more subtle*, and much *more diverse* too. So beer 'tasting' is more refined! There's no big breaths, no sucking and no spitting!

SNIFFING: Beer bunnies? Or doggy style?

Rabbits and dogs noses are constantly at work. They take *very shallow sniffs* of air, testing each against the last, to see if there are any *new aromas* nearby. That's the beer technique.

TIPS

DOGGY STYLE 'Sniff'

1. Nose into the glass
2. Take two or three little sniffs
3. Pull away and breathe in and out to clear your nose
4. Then repeat
5. Imagine inhaling a visible aroma about the size of a cherry
6. A gentle, shallow sniff
7. That's it!
   Too deep, too much, too soon – you'll miss out! Remember to swirl the glass occasionally, to release fresh aromas into the headspace.

Humans have around 6 Million nasal receptor cells, Rabbits have 100 Million and Dogs 220 Million.

FLAVOUR FILING

Once you are starting to detect one or two aromas the *difficult bit* is trying to distinguish them, because many of the aromas *come together*. So, you'll need to be able to *separate* them out.

Start mentally logging each one, or picturing something you associate it with. What does that smell *remind you of?* When you have spotted something, for example 'lemony citrus', mentally log it and *move on* to picking up something else, ignoring lemony citrus.

LENGTH OF SMELL

Aroma depends on *individual chemicals* in beer becoming *vapours* in the air. However, different aromas do this at different rates.
So the aroma profile *changes over time* for any beer, and differs between beers, depending on how volatile or vaporous they are.

TIPS

AROMA PUNCTUATION

Your aroma sensitivity becomes reduced after several sniffs.

So, set your senses back to zero with a few breaths of fresh air before re-checking for changes in aroma.

"It takes beer to make a thirst worthwhile."
German saying

We describe these different aromas as:

Flash aromas

Easily evaporated and diffuse, even at cool beer temperatures. They give the first impression of the beer, including floral, herbal and, if you're unlucky, skunky aromas from hops together with floral and sulphury smells from yeast.

Mainstay aromas

The bulk of aromas, present from the start, but more pronounced after a bit of a swirl. They are the mainstay of the beer, with fruity apples, bananas and pear drops from yeast, grainy, caramel and malty scents from cereal grains, spiciness from hops.These eventually tail off over time.

Bedrock aromas

Long-lasting aromas, still around when the beer is not fresh-poured and has warmed-up. May include caramel, toffee, nutty, chocolate and toasted characters from malt, alcoholic liqueur from yeast. Often picked up as retro-nasal aromas when the beer is warmed in the mouth.

Smell disorders:
Anosomia – lack of ability to smell
Hyposomia – decreased ability to smell
Phantosomia – 'hallucinated smell', often unpleasant
Dysomia – things smell differently than they should

FEEL IT, TASTE IT: **AT LAST!**

By now no doubt you will be desperate to have a taste, go on you have earned it. This brings us into *retro-nasal territory*, or aroma by the back door!

Beer can have *so much flavour* it is difficult for us to sort it all out. Which bits are *tastes*? Which are *aromas*? What about the *mouthfeel*? My advice is to go with what comes naturally to you, remembering that there are a limited number of taste and mouthfeel sensations, but thousands of aromas. Check out the zones of tongue sensitivity on p165.

What characteristics are most prominent to you?
They may differ from person to person.
Make sure you pass the beer from the front to back of your tongue to max the flavour effect, then rate each sensation from 1 to 5.

TIPS

ORDER OF SENSORY STIMULATION

1. Temperature and the mild pain of Carbonation are noticed first
2. The first taste sensation is salty, followed by sour, then sweet
3. Textural mouthfeel sensations include body, smooth and astringent
4. Bitterness is the last taste sensation to come in, and lasts longest too
5. Drying, if present at all, is the last mouthfeel sensation
6. Savoury (umami) and fatty tastes are rarely found in beers
7. Remember, salty sensations are easiest to detect at the tip of the tongue, sweet in the middle, sour at the sides and bitter at the back

"A fine beer may be judged with only one sip, but it's better to be thoroughly sure"
Czech Proverb

Example of a completed flavour notepad
Fill in the blanks in your notepad to create your own personal flavour reference cards

SMELL IT

	4	Hoppy/Spicy
Grainy / Malty	3.5 / 1	Roasted/ Burnt
Grassy / Nutty	1 / 0	Oily / Fatty
Sweet / Fruity	4 / 2	Sulphury
Floral / Alcohol	2 / 0	Stale / Papery
Sweet/ Caramelised	2 / 0	Medicinal
	1	Sour / Acidic
TOTAL	12.5 / 8	TOTAL

TASTE IT

Sweet	2.5 / 2	Sour
Oily / Fatty	0 / 2	Savoury
Salty	3 / 5	Initial Bitterness
	4	Lasting Bitterness
TOTAL	5.5 / 13	TOTAL

FEEL IT

Warming	3.5 / 2.5	Drying
Body	4 / 3.5	Carbonated
Smooth	3 / 3	Astringent
TOTAL	10.5 / 9	TOTAL

Copper Totals

12.5 +
5.5 +
10.5 =

Green Totals

8 +
13 +
9 =

OVERALL FLAVOUR BALANCE

28.5	GRAND TOTAL	GRAND TOTAL	30
	(SMELL IT + TASTE IT + FEEL IT)	(SMELL IT + TASTE IT + FEEL IT)	

TOTAL FLAVOUR SCORE

28.5 + 30 =

58.5

Taste disorders:
Hypogeusia – partial loss of taste
Ageusia – complete loss of taste
Parageusia – unpleasant taste
Dysgeusia – inaccurate taste

BALANCING ACT

As you repeatedly swirl & sniff at your beer, it gradually *loses carbonation and aroma*. This won't affect the basic taste characteristics but will *affect mouthfeel*, you might want to pour yourself a fresh glass.

All beers have some degree of sour and sweetness, smoothness and astringency. You will need to decide *where the balance is*. By adding up all your copper scores on one side and green scores on the other, you can determine your *perceived balance* for each beer. It *does not need to be precise*, within + or - 5 is still pretty well balanced.

Any scores against stale (papery, cardboard or leathery) aromas, oily, fatty or savoury (meaty and fishy) tastes would be considered 'off' characters and tend to imbalance the beer.

Adding together the copper and green scores from the Overall Flavour Balance will give the beer your Total Flavour Score. Then you may give it a *personal preference rating*. Irrespective of whether it's balanced or not, with a high or low Total Flavour Score, does it appeal to you?

RATE IT ★	Never again!		Disappointing		Average		Mm..Mmmm		Yes Yes YES!	
	1	2	3	4	5	6	7	8	9	10

Very quickly you will build up information on beers you have rated, and will be able to *find out why you like some beers and not others*, by noting any patterns within the scores.

Then, using the ALL **BEER** FLAVOUR GUIDE, you can *discover new styles that suit your preferences.*

TIPS

SCORING FLAVOUR BALANCE

1. Run through the whole smelling and tasting process again to confirm or revise your first impressions.
2. Look for flash aromas first, then mainstay, and bedrock aromas last.
3. Score any extremes or characters that really stand-out first.
4. Note any flavours that aren't on the balances on the back.
5. Add up copper coloured scores for SMELL IT, TASTE IT and FEEL IT from the balances and transfer the total to the Overall Flavour Balance. Do the same for green scores.
6. The sum of the Grand Total copper and green scores gives the Total Flavour Score.

Try rating one of our reference beers yourself, and compare your scores with mine.

One bottle or can could give 3 tasting servings. Why not share some new beers with your friends?

www.allbeer.co.uk will offer more interactive features plus opportunity to record and analyse your flavour notes.

SOL

IS THIS BEER OFF?

"Does YOUR beer taste alright?"
"Do you think it's MEANT to taste like this?"
We have all asked questions like these at one time or another. So, whenever you need to ask, *"Is this beer off?"*
This section will give you the answers.

Beer is classified as a *food*, so it's covered by all the usual food production and hygiene regulations, not to mention the brewer' *pride and passion*, quality assurance processes and attention to detail. We've also described some of the things that may affect beer flavour before it even gets to you.

Using the ALL **BEER** STYLE GUIDE and a bit of *judgement* you will be able to tell whether the flavours you taste are *normal and expected* for the style of beer. For instance, butterscotch may be fine in Ale but inappropriate in most Lagers. Bear in mind that just because you find an aroma or taste *strong* or *unpleasant* doesn't necessarily mean the beer is off.

TRY IT!
If you think you beer is off, complain!

"Whoever makes a poor beer is transferred to the dung hill"
City of Danzig edict 11th Century

So is the beer you taste as good as the brewer intended? More to the point *what can you do* about it if it isn't? Overleaf, we focus on the most common *off characteristics* you may come across and what might have caused them.

As beer lovers, missing out on a well-deserved and anticipated beer is disappointing, but if you believe it has a quality fault, *complaining is good*. Rejecting sub-standard beer, and telling the retailer or brewer about it, helps ensure that we all receive *top quality beer* in future.

The ALL **BEER** ANSWERS guide overleaf will help you check if your beer really is off.

The term ***ropey beer*** *relates to beer that is well below standard or off. It comes from the cloudy spirals or 'rope' formed by Acetic acid bacteria, which make beer taste like vinegar.*

DRAUGHT BEER		
FAULT SYMPTOMS	**LIKELY CAUSE**	**SUGGESTED ACTION**
Smells 'doggy'	Dirty, poorly cleaned glass, dried with a towel	Take it back, ask to have it replaced (unless it's your lipstick!)
Bubbles up the glass walls	Dirty, poorly cleaned glass, dried with a towel	
Flat, lifeless beer. Lacking carbonation & head	Poor conditioning. Gas pressure too low. Dirty glass. Lipstick on glass	
Fobbing, over-gassed beer. May also lack head	Poor conditioning. Gas pressure too high. Cooling fault. Dirty beer lines	
Fatty, oily or rancid taste and aroma	Production fault	
Cloudy beer	Disturbed cask. End of cask. Chill haze. Dirty beer lines. Infected cask or keg	A problem with the cask, keg or lines means the next pint isn't likely to be any better! Take it back. Choose another beer
Sour, acid or vinegar aroma and taste	Acetic or lactic acid bacterial infection	
Butterscotch toffee aroma in Lager	Diacetyl from poor process control or infection	
Paper, cardboard, mould or leathery aroma/ taste	Beer is old and stale. Been on sale too long. Out of BB date	
Skunky or cat pee aroma	Lightstruck beer. Drinking outdoors	Move inside. Drink a beer from a dark green or brown bottle

<table>
<tr><th colspan="5">PACKAGED BEER</th></tr>
<tr><th>FAULT SYMPTOMS</th><th colspan="2">LIKELY CAUSE</th><th colspan="2">ACTION</th></tr>
<tr><td>Sour, butterscotch, fatty or other taste fault</td><td colspan="2">Production fault or infection</td><td colspan="2">Call the brewer. Ask to have it replaced</td></tr>
<tr><td>Metallic or inky taste</td><td colspan="2">Packaging problem with can or bottle top</td><td colspan="2">Call or return to brewer. Ask to have it replaced</td></tr>
<tr><td rowspan="3">Cloudy or bitty beer</td><td rowspan="3">Protein haze, or infection</td><td>Beer is out of BB date</td><td colspan="2">Not your fault? Take it back to the retailer. Ask to have it replaced</td></tr>
<tr><td rowspan="2">Beer is within BB date</td><td>It is bottle-conditioned</td><td>Pour it steadily next time</td></tr>
<tr><td>It is not bottle-conditioned</td><td>Call or return to brewer. Ask to have it replaced</td></tr>
<tr><td rowspan="2">Paper, cardboard, mould or leathery aroma/ taste</td><td colspan="2" rowspan="2">Beer is oxidised and stale</td><td>Beer is out of BB date</td><td>Not your fault? Take it back to the retailer. Ask to have it replaced</td></tr>
<tr><td>Beer is within BB date</td><td>Call or return to brewer. Ask to have it replaced</td></tr>
<tr><td>Skunky or cat pee aroma</td><td colspan="2">Lightstruck beer. Drinking outdoors</td><td colspan="2">Move inside. Drink a beer from a dark green or brown bottle</td></tr>
</table>

Hearty Tangy Quenching
Caramel Toffee Apple Fruity
Intense Velvet
Fragrant Lavish
Elaborate Biscuity Aromatic
Rich Seasoned Konditorei
Crisp Refreshing Colossal
Clean Toasted Deceptive
Pungent Luscious Zingy

There's an appropriate beer for every drinking occasion. It's all a matter of your own personal taste and choice.

"Q"

"Everyone needs something to believe in...and I believe I'll have another beer."
W.C. Fields Comedian

SUMMARY

Thank you for reading and engaging with the ALL BEER GUIDE. I set out to create the ultimate interactive guide to the Worlds best-loved drink. I wanted to take the interactive sessions that we use with beer industry personnel, journalists and consumers to a wider audience.

photo courtesy Antonio Goard www.antoniogoard.com

Hopefully you will use the ALL BEER STYLE and FLAVOUR *guides* to open your mind and your tastebuds to a fantastic World of beer choice, and to discover some *new favourites*.

I know brewers from breweries large and small, they all share a passion for what they do. They invest time, effort and expertise in their beer. It takes many *months* to grow and select the ingredients, further weeks, months or even years to *brew and mature*. I hope that after using the ALL BEER GUIDE their investment will be fully appreciated.

I have presented you with the tools to *maximise your appreciation* of beer. Most of us have acute enough senses, they just need a bit of fine-tuning to allow you to *get the most* from your favourite beers. I hope that using the ALL BEER FLAVOUR REFERENCE CARDS and *notepad* have helped develop your tasting confidence. However you use this guide, I hope you have enjoy it.

Cheers

Alex Barlow – Master Brewer

Alex

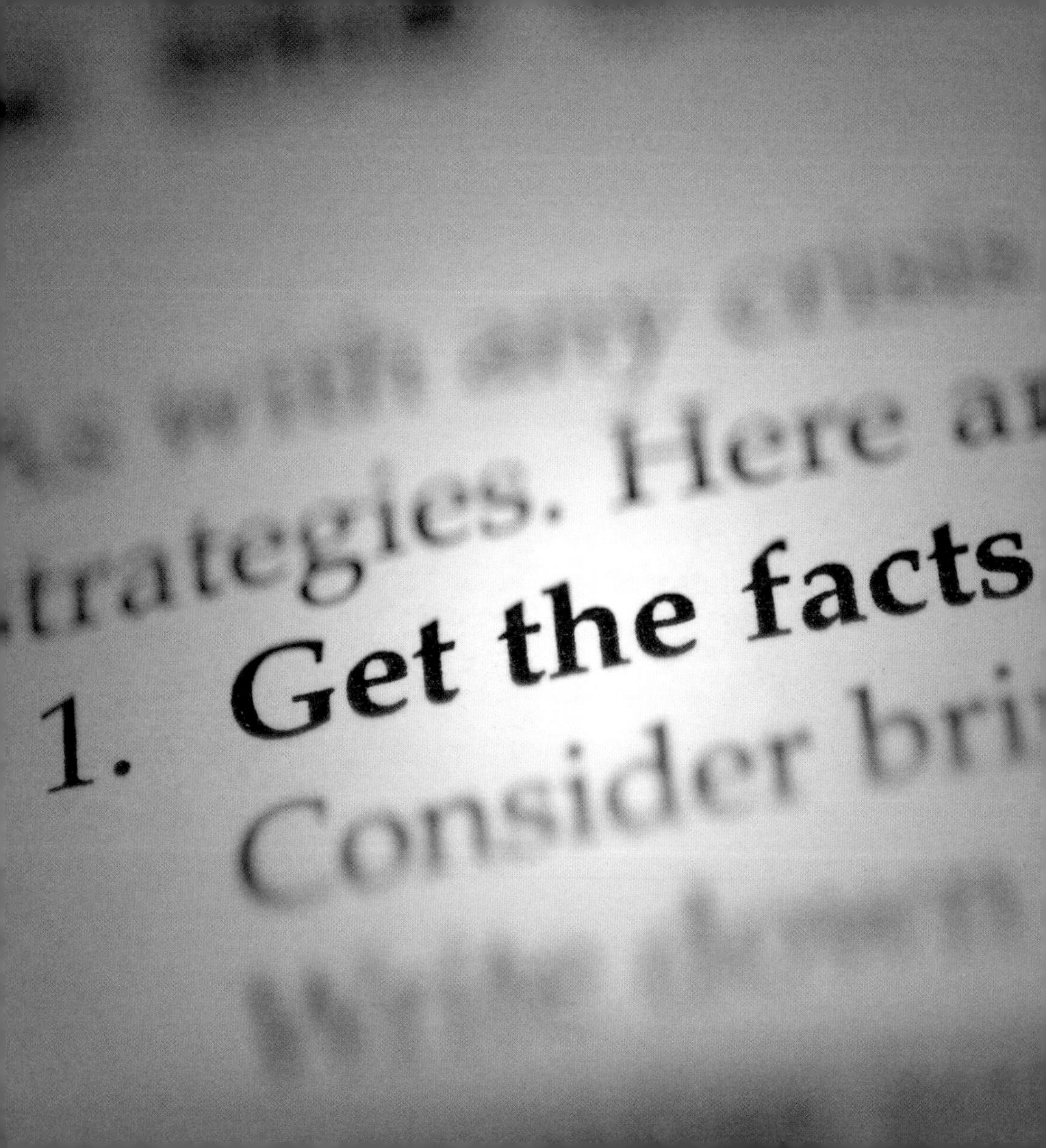

strategies. Here a

1. **Get the facts**

   Consider bri

ALL BEER
REFERENCE

A

ABi – ALL **BEER** Interactive sensory experiences.

ABV – Alcohol by Volume. Percentage measure of Alcoholic strength, per volume of fluid sampled.

Acidity – Beer acidity increases during brewing and fermentation. A fruity acidity comes from yeast in fermentation, referred to as tarte, sharp or sour.

Adjunct – Starch or sugar source used instead of malted barley. Contribute to a beer's flavour or appearance and cost of production.

Alcohol – Commonly refers to ethanol (C_2H_5OH) and also 'higher' alcohols, with more Carbon atoms, give warming, liqueur-like character to beer.

Ale – Generic name for beer brewed using top-fermenting yeast at relatively warm temperatures.

Apples – Aromas of both red and green apples may arise from yeast during the fermentation process.

Aroma – The aroma or aromatic quality refers to the smell-inducing chemicals detectable by the human nose.

Astringent – A beer mouthfeel characteristic, a grippy, cloying sensation as demonstrated by banana peel, grape pips and rhubarb or tannins in red wine or tea.

B

Balance – The harmony between the different flavour characters e.g. bitterness and sweetness, making the beer widely acceptable to drink.

Bacteria – Large group of single-celled micro organisms, existing in all Earth's habitats. Important in nutrient recycling processes within the human body, soil, water and other environments. Some bacteria can spoil beer. Harmful bacteria do not survive in beer.

Barley – Cereal crop, possessing a husk, used in beer brewing Worldwide as the sugar source for fermentation.

Beer – the generic name for alcoholic beverages fermented from grains and flavoured with hops. Include Ales, Lagers and Lambics.

Bicarbonate – (H_2CO_3) Common mineral ion in water, causing permanent hardness, contributing to dry and astringent mouthfeel.

Bitter – Primary Taste sensation. Bitterness is likened to the tang of quinine in tonic water and is produced in beer by hop resins and some dark malts. Lasting-bitterness is the lingering effect of a bitter taste. Also a style of Ale with a high hop bitterness.

Body – A beer mouthfeel characteristic relating to beer texture, fullness and complexity. Stronger, darker beers are generally higher in body. Unfermented carbohydrates contribute to the body. 'Low Carb' beers are designed to have little body.

Bohemia – Western region of the Czech Republic, famous for it's many historic brewing towns and for growing the noble Saaz (or Zatec) aroma hops.

Boiling – The process of boiling sweet wort with hops to give bitterness and aroma. It also sterilises the wort before fermentation. Traditionally performed in a copper kettle.

Bottle-Conditioned – Beer that under-goes secondary fermentation and flavour maturation in the bottle due to the continued presence or addition of yeast.

Bottom-Fermentation – A method usually associated with Lager brewing. Yeast sinks to the vessel bottom after fermentation, from where it is removed.

Bright Beer – Beer that has been filtered prior to packaging.

Broaching – The process of opening a sterile container, usually a keg or cask. Once broached it is no longer sterile.

Burnt – Pleasing, burnt flavours arise from highly kilned barley or malt in some Ales and the dominant feature of Stouts. Ranges from coffee grounds and tobacco to smoky and ashy.

Burtonisation – Generic term for any mineral salt addition to brewing water. Originally coined by British brewers adding salt to mimic Burton's Ale-suited water.

C

Calcium Sulphate – ($CaSO_4$) Commonly known as gypsum, causes temporary hardness, contributing to dry and astringent mouthfeel. Used to 'Burtonise' liquor for Ales.

Cannabinol – Tetra Hydro Cannabinol (THC) is the principal psychoactive compound in cannabis.

Caramel – A malty, caramel character is a good thing to experience in many beers. Too much can be overwhelming. Desirable in Ales, also found in some Lagers.

Carbonation – A beer mouthfeel characteristic relating to the mild pinging, pain sensation of carbon dioxide bubbles on the tongue. Relatively high or low carbonation may be detected by presence or absence of bubbles in beer.

Cask – Wood or metal container for bulk delivery of beer to pubs and bars without extra gas added. Usually associated with live beer. See below.

Cask-Conditioned Beer – 'Live beer,' where a secondary fermentation and flavour maturation occurs in the barrel due to the continued presence or addition of yeast and fermentable sugar.

Cassis – Name given to beers, usually Lambic or Oud Bruin Ale, flavoured with Blackcurrants.

Chill Haze – Temporary cloudiness that disappears when the beer is warmed.

Chloride – (Cl) Common mineral ion in water, contributing to soft, smooth and sweet taste and mouthfeel.

Chocolate – A chocolatey flavour imparted to some ales by the use of chocolate and crystal malts.

Chocolate Malt – Malt roasted at a high temperature and for a long time to produce a dark-coloured malt. It's used to give beer a darker colour and a roasted malt aroma and taste.

Citrussy – Aromatic term to describe Citrus fruit-like aromas, including lemon, lime, grapefruit and orange.

Conditioning – Maturation of beer after fermentation, with some yeast still present. Removes some unwanted flavours and haze-forming compounds, stabilises and refines flavour, and generates more carbon dioxide.

Cone – Hop 'cones' are the flower of the hop species, Humulus Lupulus, which contain resins and aromatic oils used in brewing.

Copper – The kettle in which wort is boiled with hops. Originally made of copper, after which the name is retained, even if the vessel is made with stainless steel.

Cropping – Removal of yeast after fermentation.

Crystal Malt – Partially roasted malt where sugars melt and crystalise during kilning. Used to impart colour and sweet, toffee flavours to beer.

Culture Yeast – Brewers own 'pet' yeast strains, usually DNA fingerprinted and closely guarded.

Curaçao – Dried orange peel, used to flavour drinks including Witte style Wheat beers.

Cylindro-Conical Fermenter – Tall cylindrical stainless steel fermentation vessels with a conical bottom, typically used by Lager brewers.

D

DMS – DiMethyl Sulphide. Derived from some pale Lager malts, creating vegetable-like aromas of cabbage, sweetcorn, tomatoes or beans.

Double-Decoction – Traditional mashing technique used by many Lager brewers where a portion of the mash is taken, boiled and added back to the mash to raise the temperature.

Doggy – Dirty, dog-like aroma found on poorly washed glasses or glasses stored upside-down without air circulation.

Doggy Style – ALL BEER term for the method of 'sniffing' your beer

Draught Beer – Beer dispenses from bulk casks, kegs or tanks in bars using beer lines and pumps.

Drinking Rings – Alternating lines of bubbles and spaces formed on the inside of a glass as the beer is drunk.

Dry Hopping – Addition of cone hops 'pellet' to cask beer at filling to give it a more hoppy aroma.

Drying – A beer mouthfeel characteristic: the mouth-drying, almost powdery effect of some beers. More prevalent in beers with higher alcohol and mineral salt levels.

E

Esters – Aroma compounds produced by yeast during fermentation. These give a fruity characteristic like apples, pears and bananas.

Enzymes – Naturally-occurring proteins that accelerate chemical reactions.

F

Fatty – An 'off' flavour characteristic not usually found in beers, which have almost zero fat content. May be described as 'soapy', 'oily' or 'rancid'.

Fermentation – Process of yeast reproduction where sugars are turned into alcohol and carbon dioxide, and where key flavour compounds are created.

Filtration – Brewing processes removing solids from liquids. Refers to mash filtration (removing malt husks from wort) and conditioned beer filtration (removal of yeast and protein) to create bright beer.

Finings – A purified solution of the protein collagen, often used in cask and brewery conditioning to settle yeast out of the matured beer.

Flavour Preferences – Amongst the flavours that you are able to detect, these are the ones you personally prefer, enjoy and seek out.

Floral – Aromatic character coming mainly from hops, but also from yeast. Flower-like and fragrant.

Framboise – Name given to beers, usually Lambic or Oud Bruin Ale, flavoured with raspberries.

G

Germination – Malting process during which barley sprouts and creates the enzymes necessary to convert starches into fermentable sugars.

Grassy – The aroma of fresh mown grass. Typical of lightly-germinated and kilned malt.

Green Beer – Fermented beer prior to conditioning.

Grist – Brewers term for milled malt ready for use in mashing.

Gypsum – The mineral salt calcium sulphate, found naturally in Burton water and important for flavour development in Ales.

Gushing – Phenomena of beer rushing out of an opened bottle as if it were shaken (even if it's not). Sometimes caused by a mould infection of malt.

H

Hops – The cone or flower of the hop plant. Provide bitterness and aroma, also contribute to beer foam and have preservative effects. Different varieties of hops confer different flavour characters to beers.

Hop Back – Vessel used to separate cone hops from wort after boiling, often charged with extra hops to add even more aroma.

Husk – The hard, fibrous outer layer of the barley grain, separated from wort during lautering. A source of polyphenols that can make beer cloudy.

K

Kilning – The drying or roasting of germinated barley during the malting process. The longer and higher the temperature of the kilning, the darker the malt will be. Provides much of the colour to the finished beer.

Kriek – Name given to beers, usually Lambic or Oud Bruin Ale, flavoured with cherries.

L

Lager – Generic name for beer brewed using bottom-fermenting yeast at relatively cool temperatures. The German verb, Lagern means 'to store'.

Lambic – Generic name for beers fermented with naturally occuring 'wild' yeasts from the atmosphere. Specific to the Senne valley of Belgium.

Late-hopping – The addition of extra hops at the end of wort boiling for greater hop aroma in the finished beer.

Lautering – Brewing process where sweet liquid 'wort' is separated from spent grain husks. Some breweries may combine this process with mashing.

Lauter Tun – Vessel with a slotted metal-base used to remove grain husks from the wort after mashing. Modern brewhouses may use a mash filter instead.

Lightstruck – Skunky or cat pee aroma created by 'thiol' compounds derived from hop resins subjected to sun or UV light.

Limbic System – Areas of the brain involved in emotion, motivation and emotional association with memory.

Liquor – Brewers' word for water used in the brewing process.

M

Malt – Barley that has undergone the 3-stage process of steeping, germination and kilning prior to brewing.

Malty – Flavour and aroma term relating to malt character. Also found in breakfast cereal or malted milk drinks. Common to both Lagers and Ales.

Mashing – Brewing process where milled malt grist is mixed with hot water and left to stand. Converts starches in the malt into fermentable sugars.

Mash Tun – Brewing vessel where the mashing process takes place.

Moravia – Eastern region of the Czech republic reputed for growing good malting barley.

Mouthfeel – Range of sensory terms based upon the touch or feel sense. Describe the consistency or texture of the beer in the mouth, such as 'body', 'smooth' 'astringent' and 'carbonation'.

N

Nucleation – Release of carbon dioxide gas from beer to form bubbles. Nucleation occurs at deliberate sites, or on rough or dirty surfaces of glasses containing beer.

O

Onion – Onion-like flavours can be derived from complex sulphur compounds in malt. These can range from raw onion and leek to garlic and cooked onion.

Orangey – Akin to orange peel or marmalade. Can arise from some hops and Ale yeasts. Positive, if not overwhelming.

Oxidisation – Staling of beer by oxygen. Creates flavours ranging from papery and cardboardy to mouldy and leathery.

P

Pasteurisation – Partial sterilization of a liquid, by heating for a short period, to kill any micro-organisms that may spoil it.

Peche – Name given to beers, usually Lambic or Oud Bruin Ale, flavoured with peaches.

Pitching – Adding yeast to wort to start the fermentation process.

Protein – Natural amine compounds, derived from cereals that contribute to beer body and foam. Can make beer cloudy or form chill-hazes.

R

Retro-Nasal – The smelling experience caused by release of aromas, often the heavier ones, into your nose after taking food or drink into your mouth.

Rough Beer – Fermented beer, yet to be filtered for packaging.

S

Saaz – Also known by its Czech name, Zatec. A noble aroma hop, widely used amongst some of the World's best Lager brewers.

Salty – Primary taste sensation based upon receptors sensitive to sodium ions. Used as a tasting term to describe a range of mineral-salt flavours.

Savoury – Primary taste sensation based upon receptors sensitive to glutamate-rich foods such as fish, meats and monosodium glutamate. Generally absent from beer.

Smooth – A beer mouthfeel characteristic relating to texture, influenced by relative levels of mineral salts, large sugars and proteins in beer.

Soporific – Sleep inducing.

Sour – Primary Taste sensation based upon receptors sensitive to hydrogen ions. Describes an acidic character, a tarte sharpness found in some beers.

Spicy – This clove-like flavour may come from the grains as well as a spicy hop character.

Starch – Large complex sugars naturally found in grains such as barley, wheat, maize & rice. Broken down by enzymes to simple sugars for yeast to ferment.

Steeping – The first malting process, where barley is soaked in water to induce break dormancy and start germination.

Struck Match – Sulphury, just-struck match, aroma derived from yeast.

Sweet – Primary taste sensation associated with sugars and some proteins. A characteristic common to all beers to a greater or lesser degree, from malt or cereal derived sugars.

T

Thiols – Compounds containing a sulphydryl (SH) group of sulphur & hydrogen, also known as mercaptans. Responsible for foul smells like skunk, faeces and rotting flesh and more pleasant smells like garlic & grapefruit.

Toasted – A characteristic of dark malts, transferred to darker beers using them such as Milds, Porters, Stouts and dark Lagers.

Toffee – A malt characteristic close to caramel, but stronger and darker, derived from carapils, ale and crystal malts found mainly in Ales.

Top-fermenting – A method usually associated with Ales. Yeast rises and collects as a crust on the top of the beer after fermentation, from where it is collected.

Trub – The vegetable matter from hops together with proteins, left after boiling wort.

Tun – Generic name for large brewing vessels eg. mash tun, lauter tun.

U

Umami – see Savoury.

V

Vanilla – Malt-derived flavour formed in some beers during ageing, it brings a pleasing aroma to some beer varieties.

Volatile – Substances, in our terms flavour substances, easily evaporated at normal temperatures.

W

Warming – A beer mouthfeel characteristic brought about by Ethanol and a range of higher alcohols produced by yeast during fermentation. Higher concentrations of alcohol produce a chemical warming sensation.

Wheat – Cereal grain commonly used in smaller amounts as a brewing starch source, or in larger amounts as a beer style in its own right. Wheat proteins help beer head formation.

Widget – Small plastic or metal device located inside a can or bottle that, on opening, squirts a jet of nitrogen bubbles into the beer, mimicking draught beer dispense, and forming a smooth creamy head.

Wort – The sweet solution of malt sugars after separation from malt husks.

Whirlpool – A brewing vessel that uses a swirling action to separate trub from wort after boiling.

Y

Yeast – Common name for brewers' Saccharomyces yeast strains. A single-celled fungus that creates beer by fermenting wort sugars into alcohol and carbon dioxide and releasing flavour compounds.

Yeast-bite – Excessive yeast sharpness, a savoury taste sensation unusual in most beers. Can come from extended contact with yeast, and is more typical of cask or bottled-conditioned beers.

Yorkshire Stone Squares – Traditional stone-sided, often slate, fermentation vessels, once common in Ale breweries in Yorkshire, England.

#1 – WATER (from p.19)

Usually there is very little difference in TASTE, though some waters may be a little more SALTY than others, mainly due to the levels of sodium and potassium salts. Much of the difference is usually in how they FEEL in your mouth. Some are drier or more CHALKY, due to the sulphate and bicarbonate salts. Chloride makes the water feel more smooth, sweet and full.

ABi

#2 – MALT (from p.21)

TASTE SAMPLE	SENSORY EXPERIENCE
BARLEY	Very hard and has little taste, just a bit floury
LAGER MALT	Softer with a light malty taste, slightly grassy or grainy
ALE MALT	Softer with a sweeter more biscuity, malty taste
CRYSTAL	Crunchy crystals with a bittersweet toffee taste
CHOCOLATE MALT	Powdery with a burnt toast, acrid coffee taste

#3 – HOPS
(see Hop Card in ALL BEER EXPERIENCE PACK)

#4 – YEAST (from p.29)

Yeast itself has a savoury taste and some quite sulphury aromas. The sediment of a bottle-conditioned or wheat beer can give you an idea of what it's like. Marmite is derived from yeast and is about as intense as the savoury, meaty taste sensation gets without any meat present.

#5 – SEE IT (from p.54)

	LAGER	ALE	STOUT
COLOUR	Pale, straw, gold	Amber, bronze, mahogany, brown	In very bright light – deep scarlet red Normal light – burnt black
CLARITY	Brilliant, sparkling	Clear, bright, translucent	Appears ebony-black, but semi-opaque
CARBONATION	Ample, fine, lively, effervescent	Large, loose, infrequent	Tiny, surging, swirling bubbles
CLING/ HEAD	Fine, light, white, sparkling	Full, creamy, thick, lasting	Coffee, creamy, velvety, lasting

#6 – HEAR IT (as per p.56)

ABi

#7 – SMELL IT (as per p.60/61)

for guidance only

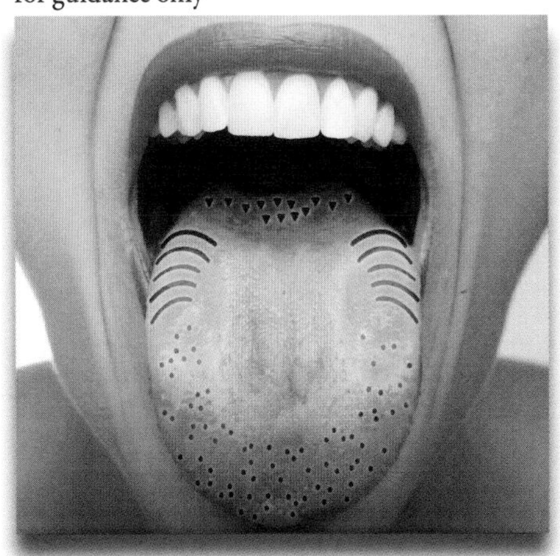

#8 – TASTE IT (from p.66)

TASTE SAMPLE	SENSORY EXPERIENCE
SWEET – SUGAR	Sweet sensations are usually most pronounced on the front & sides of the tongue
SALTY – TABLE SALT	Salty is picked up right at the tip of the tongue and some at the sides
SOUR – LEMON	Sharp, sour acidic sensations are picked up most as a tingle down the sides of the tongue
BITTER – TONIC	Bitterness is sensed most at the back of the tongue
SAVOURY – BOVRIL	Savoury tastes are picked up in most areas

#9 – FEEL IT (from p.69)

	MOUTHFEEL	SENSORY EXPERIENCE
TEMPERATURE	WARMING	At 5% it's very weak vodka, but that of 'premium' strength beer. Gets progressively stronger, finally burning across the whole surface of the mouth, not just the tongue
	COOLING	The menthol of the mint gives a false cooling effect, the opposite of the vodka's warming effect
BODY	THIN	Water feels thin. It has no body.
	FULL-BODIED	Milk has more body. Skimmed Milk has least, followed by Semi-skimmed then Full Fat milk. Cream has more body still. There is no fat in beer. But more malt carbohydrates and sugars create more body.
TEXTURE	SMOOTH	Licking a sliced banana gives the ultimate lubricated, silky smooth texture
	ASTRINGENT	Green banana skin gives a harsh, mouth-puckering tongue-roughening sensation. The opposite of smoothness a wet tea bag or grape pips have a similar effect
	CARBONATION	A harsh biting, tingling sensation. How long did you manage? Some people struggle to hold on for 5s. 10-15s is about average. Up to 30s and you're probably a raw chilli eater!
	DRYING	(No ABi, as tricky to do safely at home.) Experienced as a increasingly dry, powdery sensation.

#10 – COMBINED FLAVOURS (from p.71)

STIMULUS	AROMAS	TASTES	MOUTHFEEL
VODKA/ GIN & TONIC	Liqueur-like higher alcohols; citrus; juniper; herbal	Sweet; sour; bitter	Cold; carbonated; smooth; drying; warming
MILK CHOCOLATE	Chocolate; creamy	Sweet; fatty; salty	Smooth; full-bodied
70% DARK CHOCOLATE	Intense chocolate; roasted	Less sweet; less fatty; bitter	Often less smooth, less body, more drying

ABi Some items used in ABi's # 1 to 10

✓ STORE CUPBOARD LIST

- ☐ Mineral water
- ☐ Marmite, Bovril or Beef stock cube
- ☐ Vodka, Bacardi or Gin (clear spirit)
- ☐ Milk, Single and /or Double cream
- ☐ Green Banana or wet tea bag
- ☐ Cola, or other fizzy soft drink
- ☐ Sugar
- ☐ Table Salt
- ☐ Lemon juice
- ☐ Tonic water
- ☐ Green apple e.g. Granny Smith
- ☐ Red apple e.g. Cox, Braeburn or Washington
- ☐ Ripe banana
- ☐ Hard-boiled egg
- ☐ Half a dozen just-struck matches
- ☐ Schnapps or fruit liqueur
- ☐ Weetabix or Shredded Wheat
- ☐ Malt extract, Horlicks or malted milk biscuit
- ☐ Tin of Sweetcorn
- ☐ Vanilla pod or essence
- ☐ 70% Dark Chocolate
- ☐ Milk Chocolate
- ☐ Handful of Toffees or Fudge
- ☐ Cup of black coffee
- ☐ Slice of burnt toast
- ☐ Jar of mixed herbs
- ☐ Dried grass cuttings, hay or straw
- ☐ Lemon, or Lime or Pink Grapefruit
- ☐ Orange marmalade
- ☐ Fresh cut flowers

Ref#	Subject	Author	Publication	Date
1	Beer Volumes	WARC	World Drinks Trends 2003	2005
2	Ale	Random House	Random House Unabridged Dictionary, © Random House, Inc. 2006.	2006
3	Sense of smell	Diracdelta.co.uk	Diracdelta.co.uk Science & Engineering Encyclodpedia	2007
4	The Proust Effect: Involuntary memory response	Marcel Proust	In search of lost time	c.1913
5	Womens acute sense of smell.	Hughes et al.	Climacteric	2002, June; w5 (2): 140-150
6	Supertasters	Bartoshuk	The science radio show, Radio National, USA	9th June 1997 & November 2003
7	Taste buds	Tim Jacobs	www.cf.ac.uk/biosi/staff/jacob/teaching/sensory/taste.html	March 2007

BIBLIOGRAPHY

RW Moncreif, The Chemical Senses, 3rd Edition, Leonard Hill, London 1967

Dr. Alan Hirsch, Taste Treatment & Research Foundation, Chicago

Bowman & Rand, Textbook of Pharmacology

Dr. Susan Schiffman, Chicago Tribune

Bone & Allen, Psychological Science

AT Austin, Brain Mind & Language, NLP

Canadian Institute of Health Research

Miles & Jenkins, Odour Memory

Monell, Chemical Senses Centre

Society for Neuro-Science

Today's Chemist at Work

Schreiber, F. (1992). Aging and the senses. In J. E. Birren, R. B. Sloane, & G. D. Cohen (Eds.), Handbook of mental health and aging. San Diego: Academic Press Inc.

Schiffman, S. (1977). Food recognition by the elderly. Journal of Gerontology, 32 (5), 586-592.

Tim Jacob, Cardiff University, Sensory / taste

www.bbc.co.uk

www.wikipaedia.com

www.medical-news.net

www.innerbody.com

Acknowledgements

Scott Wilson and Jane Hall for opportunities and enthusiasm to enlighten others about beer.

Music and Portrait photographer, Andy Fallon www.andyfallon.co.uk

Antonio Goard, Photographer www.antoniogoard.com

International Cartoonist & Illustrator, Ian Baker ('Cat Pee') ianbakercartoons.co.uk

Artist Martin Beal ('Chicha') martinbealart.co.uk

Classic comic strip veteran Mychailo Kazybrid ('Fido homebrew')
Character Creation, mychailo@btinternet.com

Hannah and Ben at the Devonshire Cat, Sheffield, UK
for well informed bar staff and allowing photography.

Champs Sports Bar, Sheffield, UK ('busy bar') for allowing photography.

Banja Luka Pivovara, for allowing photography.

Yeast microscopic photography courtesy of Dr Chris Boulton.

Helen Thomson, many thanks for all your help.

Julie, Jamie & Frank, thanks for the insightful comments.

Phil & Nick at Curve Digital Ltd. "Thanks for everything!"

To all the brewers, past and present, I have worked, learned and shared a beer with. Thank you.

ABOUT ALEX

Alex was brought up in Chester, Northwest England and in Africa.

His 25 years experience in brewing started as a bar and cellarman in his local pub, before studying for his two Medical Sciences degrees.

He learned his brewing skills at breweries around the UK, becoming the youngest qualified Master Brewer, before moving roles to police beer quality in the pubs and clubs of Yorkshire and North East England.

He became the first Englishman to manage a Czech brewery, and developed two new beer brands, whilst gaining a taste for European beers. He has brewed, sold and marketed some of the UK's leading brands.

Alex is an independent beer flavour consultant, presenter and sommelier, creating and presenting beer flavour experience events for UK and European brewers, publications like The Times and Arena, pub groups, supermarkets and beer consumers.

Alex and his family live in Sheffield. When he isn't tasting, writing or talking about beer, he loves to cook, listen to music, and walk or cycle in the nearby hills.

Alex is a member of the

IBD – Institute of Brewing & Distilling (International),

MBAA – Master Brewers Association of the Americas,

BGBW – British Guild of Beer Writers.

ALL BEER
FLAVOUR NOTEPAD

ALL **BEER** NOTEPAD

Chart your own experience's to understand and develop your own beer preferences

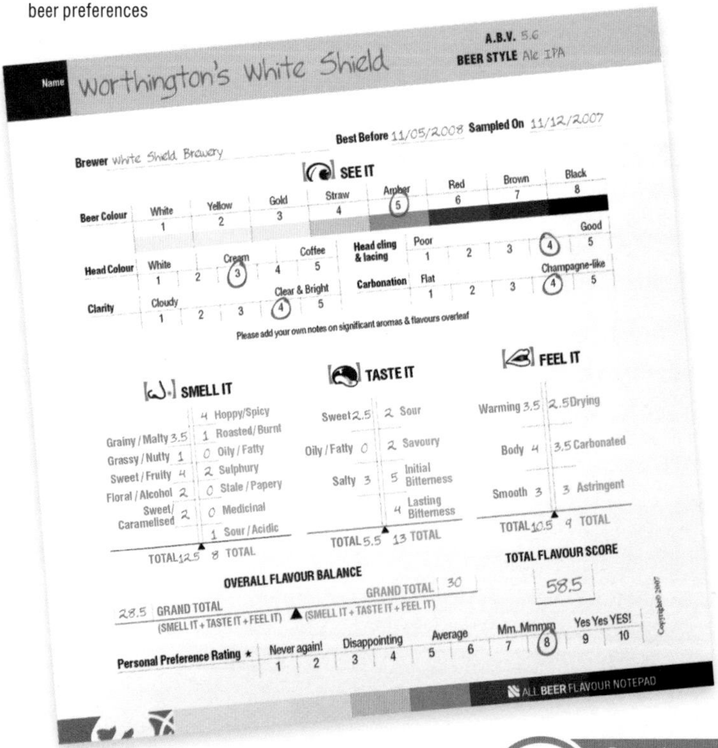

Name Worthington's White Shield

A.B.V. 5.6
BEER STYLE Ale IPA

Brewer White Shield Brewery
Best Before 11/05/2008 Sampled On 11/12/2007

SEE IT

Beer Colour	White	Yellow	Gold	Straw	Amber	Red	Brown	Black
	1	2	3	4	(5)	6	7	8

Head Colour: White 1, 2, Cream (3), 4, Coffee 5
Head cling & lacing: Poor 1, 2, 3, (4), Good 5
Clarity: Cloudy 1, 2, 3, (4), Clear & Bright 5
Carbonation: Flat 1, 2, 3, (4), Champagne-like 5

Please add your own notes on significant aromas & flavours overleaf

SMELL IT

		4	Hoppy/Spicy
Grainy / Malty	3.5	1	Roasted/ Burnt
Grassy / Nutty	1	0	Oily / Fatty
Sweet / Fruity	4	2	Sulphury
Floral / Alcohol	2	0	Stale / Papery
Sweet/ Caramelised	2	0	Medicinal
		1	Sour / Acidic
TOTAL	12.5	8	TOTAL

TASTE IT

Sweet	2.5	2	Sour
Oily / Fatty	0	2	Savoury
Salty	3	5	Initial Bitterness
		4	Lasting Bitterness
TOTAL	5.5	13	TOTAL

FEEL IT

Warming	3.5	2.5	Drying
Body	4	3.5	Carbonated
Smooth	3	3	Astringent
TOTAL	10.5	9	TOTAL

OVERALL FLAVOUR BALANCE

28.5 GRAND TOTAL (SMELL IT + TASTE IT + FEEL IT) ▲ GRAND TOTAL 30 (SMELL IT + TASTE IT + FEEL IT)

TOTAL FLAVOUR SCORE 58.5

Personal Preference Rating ★ Never again! 1, 2, Disappointing 3, 4, Average 5, 6, Mm..Mmmm 7, (8), Yes Yes YES! 9, 10

Copyright© 2007

ALL BEER FLAVOUR NOTEPAD

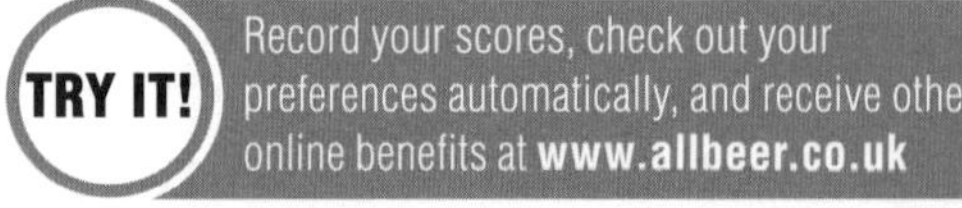

ame

A.B.V.

BEER STYLE

rewer .... **Best Before** .... **Sampled On** ....

SEE IT

eer Colour	White	Yellow	Gold	Straw	Amber	Red	Brown	Black
	1	2	3	4	5	6	7	8

ead Colour	White		Cream		Coffee
	1	2	3	4	5

Head cling & lacing	Poor				Good
	1	2	3	4	5

larity	Cloudy				Clear & Bright
	1	2	3	4	5

Carbonation	Flat				Champagne-like
	1	2	3	4	5

Please add your own notes on significant aromas & flavours overleaf

SMELL IT

	Hoppy/Spicy
Grainy / Malty	Roasted/ Burnt
Grassy / Nutty	Oily / Fatty
Sweet / Fruity	Sulphury
Floral / Alcohol	Stale / Papery
Sweet/ Caramelised	Medicinal
	Sour / Acidic
TOTAL	TOTAL

TASTE IT

Sweet	Sour
Oily / Fatty	Savoury
Salty	Initial Bitterness
	Lasting Bitterness
TOTAL	TOTAL

FEEL IT

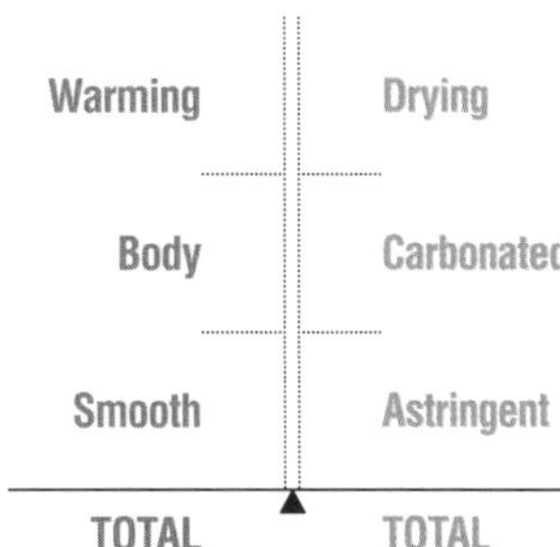

OVERALL FLAVOUR BALANCE

GRAND TOTAL (SMELL IT + TASTE IT + FEEL IT) ▲ GRAND TOTAL (SMELL IT + TASTE IT + FEEL IT)

TOTAL FLAVOUR SCORE

ATE IT ★	Never again!		Disappointing		Average		Mm..Mmmm		Yes Yes YES!	
	1	2	3	4	5	6	7	8	9	10

me

A.B.V.

BEER STYLE

ewer | Best Before | Sampled On

SEE IT

er Colour	White	Yellow	Gold	Straw	Amber	Red	Brown	Black
	1	2	3	4	5	6	7	8

ad Colour	White		Cream		Coffee
	1	2	3	4	5

Head cling & lacing	Poor				Good
	1	2	3	4	5

arity	Cloudy				Clear & Bright
	1	2	3	4	5

Carbonation	Flat				Champagne-like
	1	2	3	4	5

Please add your own notes on significant aromas & flavours overleaf

SMELL IT

	Hoppy/Spicy
Grainy / Malty	Roasted/ Burnt
Grassy / Nutty	Oily / Fatty
Sweet / Fruity	Sulphury
Floral / Alcohol	Stale / Papery
Sweet/ Caramelised	Medicinal
	Sour / Acidic
TOTAL	TOTAL

TASTE IT

Sweet	Sour
Oily / Fatty	Savoury
Salty	Initial Bitterness
	Lasting Bitterness
TOTAL	TOTAL

FEEL IT

Warming	Drying
Body	Carbonated
Smooth	Astringent
TOTAL	TOTAL

OVERALL FLAVOUR BALANCE

GRAND TOTAL (SMELL IT + TASTE IT + FEEL IT)	GRAND TOTAL (SMELL IT + TASTE IT + FEEL IT)

TOTAL FLAVOUR SCORE

ATE IT ★	Never again!		Disappointing		Average		Mm..Mmmm		Yes Yes YES!	
	1	2	3	4	5	6	7	8	9	10

Name

A.B.V.

BEER STYLE

Brewer .... **Best Before** .... **Sampled On** ....

SEE IT

Beer Colour	White	Yellow	Gold	Straw	Amber	Red	Brown	Black
	1	2	3	4	5	6	7	8

Head Colour	White		Cream		Coffee
	1	2	3	4	5

Head cling & lacing	Poor				Good
	1	2	3	4	5

Clarity	Cloudy				Clear & Bright
	1	2	3	4	5

Carbonation	Flat				Champagne-like
	1	2	3	4	5

Please add your own notes on significant aromas & flavours overleaf

OVERALL FLAVOUR BALANCE

GRAND TOTAL (SMELL IT + TASTE IT + FEEL IT) | GRAND TOTAL (SMELL IT + TASTE IT + FEEL IT)

TOTAL FLAVOUR SCORE

RATE IT ★	Never again!		Disappointing		Average		Mm..Mmmm		Yes Yes YES!	
	1	2	3	4	5	6	7	8	9	10

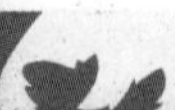
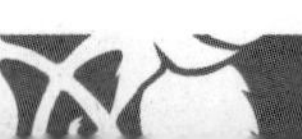

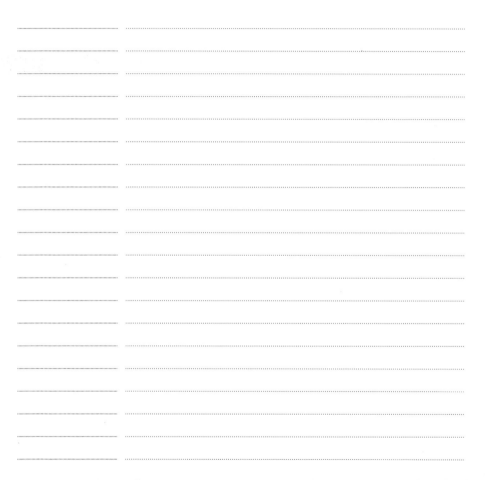

Name

A.B.V.

BEER STYLE

Brewer .... **Best Before** .... **Sampled On** ....

SEE IT

Beer Colour	White	Yellow	Gold	Straw	Amber	Red	Brown	Black
	1	2	3	4	5	6	7	8

Head Colour	White		Cream		Coffee
	1	2	3	4	5

Head cling & lacing	Poor				Good
	1	2	3	4	5

Clarity	Cloudy				Clear & Bright
	1	2	3	4	5

Carbonation	Flat				Champagne-like
	1	2	3	4	5

Please add your own notes on significant aromas & flavours overleaf

SMELL IT

	Hoppy/Spicy
Grainy / Malty	Roasted/ Burnt
Grassy / Nutty	Oily / Fatty
Sweet / Fruity	Sulphury
Floral / Alcohol	Stale / Papery
Sweet/ Caramelised	Medicinal
	Sour / Acidic
TOTAL	TOTAL

TASTE IT

Sweet	Sour
Oily / Fatty	Savoury
Salty	Initial Bitterness
	Lasting Bitterness
TOTAL	TOTAL

FEEL IT

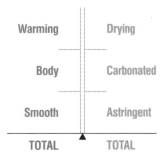

Warming	Drying
Body	Carbonated
Smooth	Astringent
TOTAL	TOTAL

OVERALL FLAVOUR BALANCE

GRAND TOTAL (SMELL IT + TASTE IT + FEEL IT)	GRAND TOTAL (SMELL IT + TASTE IT + FEEL IT)

TOTAL FLAVOUR SCORE

RATE IT ★	Never again!		Disappointing		Average		Mm..Mmmm		Yes Yes YES!	
	1	2	3	4	5	6	7	8	9	10

Name

A.B.V.

BEER STYLE

Brewer .... Best Before .... Sampled On ....

SEE IT

Beer Colour	White	Yellow	Gold	Straw	Amber	Red	Brown	Black
	1	2	3	4	5	6	7	8

Head Colour	White		Cream		Coffee
	1	2	3	4	5

Head cling & lacing	Poor				Good
	1	2	3	4	5

Clarity	Cloudy				Clear & Bright
	1	2	3	4	5

Carbonation	Flat				Champagne-like
	1	2	3	4	5

Please add your own notes on significant aromas & flavours overleaf

SMELL IT

TASTE IT

FEEL IT

SMELL IT: Grainy / Malty; Grassy / Nutty; Sweet / Fruity; Floral / Alcohol; Sweet/ Caramelised | Hoppy/Spicy; Roasted/ Burnt; Oily / Fatty; Sulphury; Stale / Papery; Medicinal; Sour / Acidic

TOTAL | TOTAL

TASTE IT: Sweet; Oily / Fatty; Salty | Sour; Savoury; Initial Bitterness; Lasting Bitterness

TOTAL | TOTAL

FEEL IT: Warming; Body; Smooth | Drying; Carbonated; Astringent

TOTAL | TOTAL

OVERALL FLAVOUR BALANCE

GRAND TOTAL (SMELL IT + TASTE IT + FEEL IT) | GRAND TOTAL (SMELL IT + TASTE IT + FEEL IT)

TOTAL FLAVOUR SCORE

RATE IT ★	Never again!		Disappointing		Average		Mm..Mmmm		Yes Yes YES!	
	1	2	3	4	5	6	7	8	9	10

Name | A.B.V. | BEER STYLE

Brewer | Best Before | Sampled On

SEE IT

Beer Colour	White	Yellow	Gold	Straw	Amber	Red	Brown	Black
	1	2	3	4	5	6	7	8

Head Colour	White		Cream		Coffee
	1	2	3	4	5

Head cling & lacing	Poor				Good
	1	2	3	4	5

Clarity	Cloudy			Clear & Bright	
	1	2	3	4	5

Carbonation	Flat			Champagne-like	
	1	2	3	4	5

Please add your own notes on significant aromas & flavours overleaf

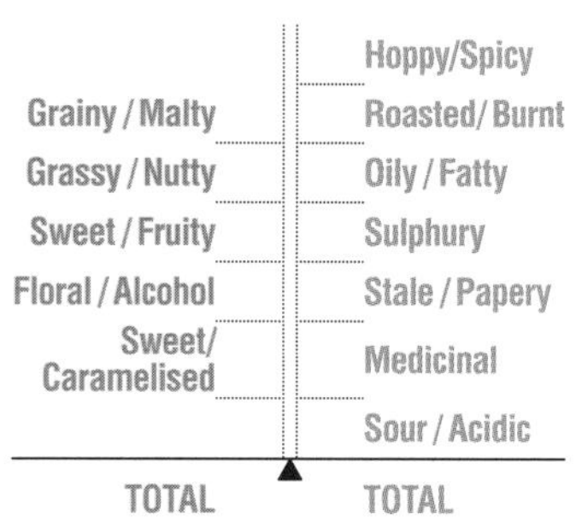

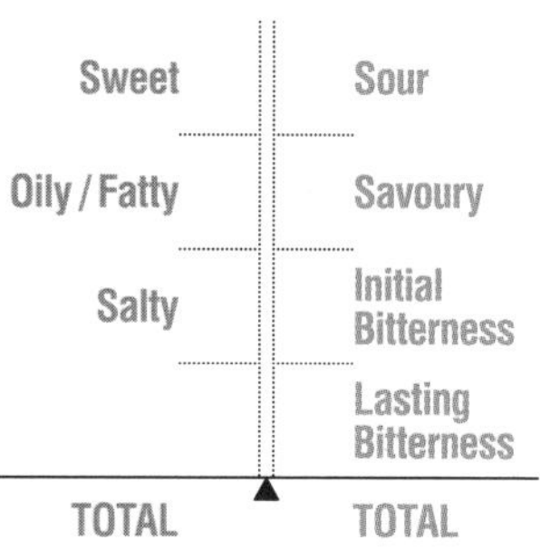

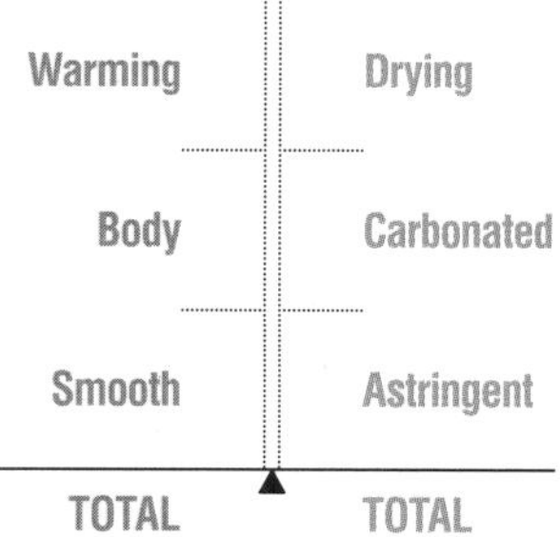

OVERALL FLAVOUR BALANCE

GRAND TOTAL (SMELL IT + TASTE IT + FEEL IT) | GRAND TOTAL (SMELL IT + TASTE IT + FEEL IT)

TOTAL FLAVOUR SCORE

RATE IT ★	Never again!		Disappointing		Average		Mm..Mmmm		Yes Yes YES!	
	1	2	3	4	5	6	7	8	9	10

Name		A.B.V.
		BEER STYLE

Brewer .... Best Before .... Sampled On ....

SEE IT

Beer Colour	White	Yellow	Gold	Straw	Amber	Red	Brown	Black
	1	2	3	4	5	6	7	8

Head Colour	White		Cream		Coffee
	1	2	3	4	5

Head cling & lacing	Poor				Good
	1	2	3	4	5

Clarity	Cloudy				Clear & Bright
	1	2	3	4	5

Carbonation	Flat				Champagne-like
	1	2	3	4	5

Please add your own notes on significant aromas & flavours overleaf

SMELL IT

	Hoppy/Spicy
Grainy / Malty	Roasted/ Burnt
Grassy / Nutty	Oily / Fatty
Sweet / Fruity	Sulphury
Floral / Alcohol	Stale / Papery
Sweet/ Caramelised	Medicinal
	Sour / Acidic
TOTAL	TOTAL

TASTE IT

Sweet	Sour
Oily / Fatty	Savoury
Salty	Initial Bitterness
	Lasting Bitterness
TOTAL	TOTAL

FEEL IT

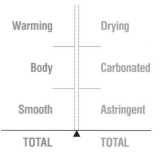

Warming	Drying
Body	Carbonated
Smooth	Astringent
TOTAL	TOTAL

OVERALL FLAVOUR BALANCE

GRAND TOTAL (SMELL IT + TASTE IT + FEEL IT) | GRAND TOTAL (SMELL IT + TASTE IT + FEEL IT)

TOTAL FLAVOUR SCORE

RATE IT ★	Never again!		Disappointing		Average		Mm..Mmmm		Yes Yes YES!	
	1	2	3	4	5	6	7	8	9	10

ame	A.B.V.
BEER STYLE

rewer .... **Best Before** .... **Sampled On** ....

SEE IT

eer Colour	White	Yellow	Gold	Straw	Amber	Red	Brown	Black
	1	2	3	4	5	6	7	8

ead Colour	White		Cream		Coffee
	1	2	3	4	5

Head cling & lacing	Poor				Good
	1	2	3	4	5

larity	Cloudy				Clear & Bright
	1	2	3	4	5

Carbonation	Flat				Champagne-like
	1	2	3	4	5

Please add your own notes on significant aromas & flavours overleaf

SMELL IT

	Hoppy/Spicy
Grainy / Malty	Roasted/ Burnt
Grassy / Nutty	Oily / Fatty
Sweet / Fruity	Sulphury
Floral / Alcohol	Stale / Papery
Sweet/ Caramelised	Medicinal
	Sour / Acidic
TOTAL	TOTAL

TASTE IT

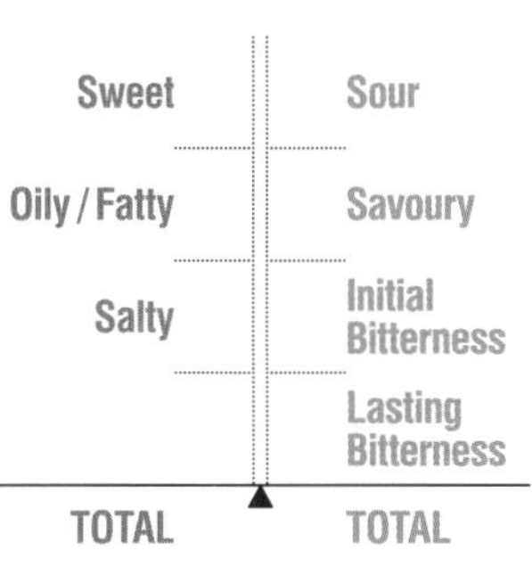

FEEL IT

Warming	Drying
Body	Carbonated
Smooth	Astringent
TOTAL	TOTAL

OVERALL FLAVOUR BALANCE

GRAND TOTAL (SMELL IT + TASTE IT + FEEL IT) | GRAND TOTAL (SMELL IT + TASTE IT + FEEL IT)

TOTAL FLAVOUR SCORE

RATE IT ★	Never again!		Disappointing		Average		Mm..Mmmm		Yes Yes YES!	
	1	2	3	4	5	6	7	8	9	10

Name	A.B.V. BEER STYLE

Brewer .... **Best Before** .... **Sampled On** ....

SEE IT

Beer Colour	White	Yellow	Gold	Straw	Amber	Red	Brown	Black
	1	2	3	4	5	6	7	8

Head Colour	White		Cream		Coffee
	1	2	3	4	5

Head cling & lacing	Poor				Good
	1	2	3	4	5

Clarity	Cloudy				Clear & Bright
	1	2	3	4	5

Carbonation	Flat				Champagne-like
	1	2	3	4	5

Please add your own notes on significant aromas & flavours overleaf

SMELL IT

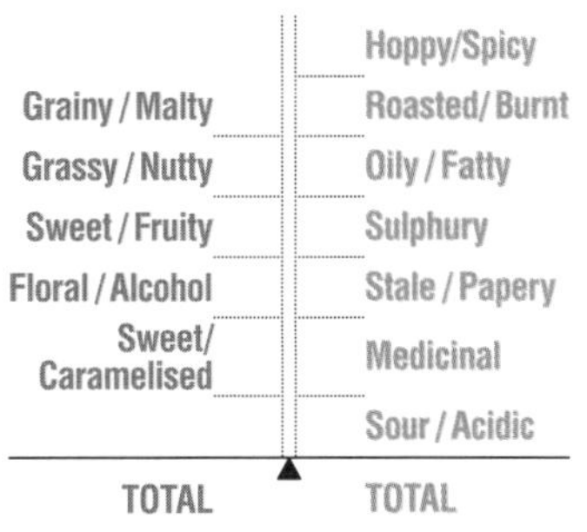

TASTE IT

FEEL IT

Warming | Drying

Body | Carbonated

Smooth | Astringent

TOTAL | TOTAL

OVERALL FLAVOUR BALANCE

GRAND TOTAL (SMELL IT + TASTE IT + FEEL IT) | GRAND TOTAL (SMELL IT + TASTE IT + FEEL IT)

TOTAL FLAVOUR SCORE

RATE IT ★	Never again!		Disappointing		Average		Mm..Mmmm		Yes Yes YES!	
	1	2	3	4	5	6	7	8	9	10

Name **A.B.V.**

BEER STYLE

Brewer .... **Best Before** .... **Sampled On** ....

SEE IT

Beer Colour	White	Yellow	Gold	Straw	Amber	Red	Brown	Black
	1	2	3	4	5	6	7	8

Head Colour	White		Cream		Coffee
	1	2	3	4	5

Head cling & lacing	Poor				Good
	1	2	3	4	5

Clarity	Cloudy				Clear & Bright
	1	2	3	4	5

Carbonation	Flat				Champagne-like
	1	2	3	4	5

Please add your own notes on significant aromas & flavours overleaf

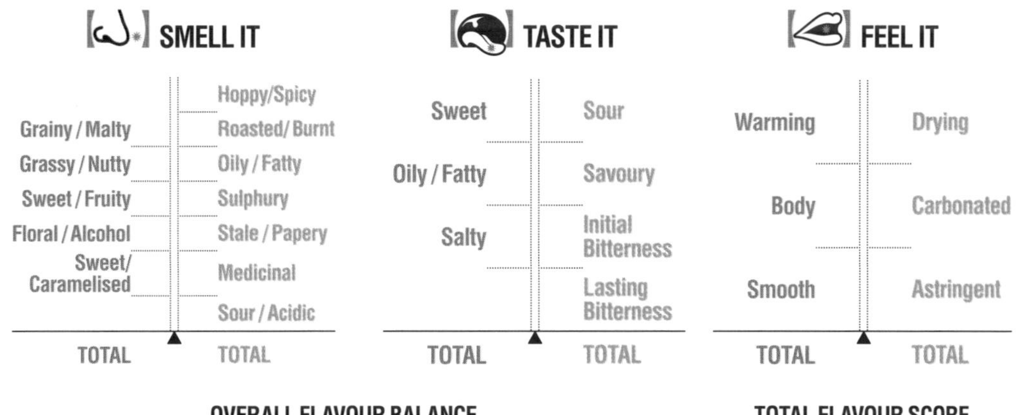

SMELL IT

Grainy / Malty
Grassy / Nutty
Sweet / Fruity
Floral / Alcohol
Sweet/ Caramelised

Hoppy/Spicy
Roasted/ Burnt
Oily / Fatty
Sulphury
Stale / Papery
Medicinal
Sour / Acidic

TOTAL TOTAL

TASTE IT

Sweet
Oily / Fatty
Salty

Sour
Savoury
Initial Bitterness
Lasting Bitterness

TOTAL TOTAL

FEEL IT

Warming
Body
Smooth

Drying
Carbonated
Astringent

TOTAL TOTAL

OVERALL FLAVOUR BALANCE

GRAND TOTAL (SMELL IT + TASTE IT + FEEL IT) GRAND TOTAL (SMELL IT + TASTE IT + FEEL IT)

TOTAL FLAVOUR SCORE

RATE IT ★	Never again!		Disappointing		Average		Mm..Mmmm		Yes Yes YES!	
	1	2	3	4	5	6	7	8	9	10

Name

A.B.V.

BEER STYLE

Brewer .... Best Before .... Sampled On ....

SEE IT

Beer Colour	White	Yellow	Gold	Straw	Amber	Red	Brown	Black
	1	2	3	4	5	6	7	8

Head Colour	White		Cream		Coffee
	1	2	3	4	5

Head cling & lacing	Poor				Good
	1	2	3	4	5

Clarity	Cloudy				Clear & Bright
	1	2	3	4	5

Carbonation	Flat				Champagne-like
	1	2	3	4	5

Please add your own notes on significant aromas & flavours overleaf

OVERALL FLAVOUR BALANCE

GRAND TOTAL (SMELL IT + TASTE IT + FEEL IT) — GRAND TOTAL (SMELL IT + TASTE IT + FEEL IT)

TOTAL FLAVOUR SCORE

RATE IT ★	Never again!		Disappointing		Average		Mm..Mmmm		Yes Yes YES!	
	1	2	3	4	5	6	7	8	9	10

Name

A.B.V.

BEER STYLE

Brewer .... **Best Before** .... **Sampled On** ....

SEE IT

Beer Colour	White	Yellow	Gold	Straw	Amber	Red	Brown	Black
	1	2	3	4	5	6	7	8

Head Colour	White		Cream		Coffee
	1	2	3	4	5

Head cling & lacing	Poor				Good
	1	2	3	4	5

Clarity	Cloudy				Clear & Bright
	1	2	3	4	5

Carbonation	Flat				Champagne-like
	1	2	3	4	5

Please add your own notes on significant aromas & flavours overleaf

SMELL IT

TASTE IT

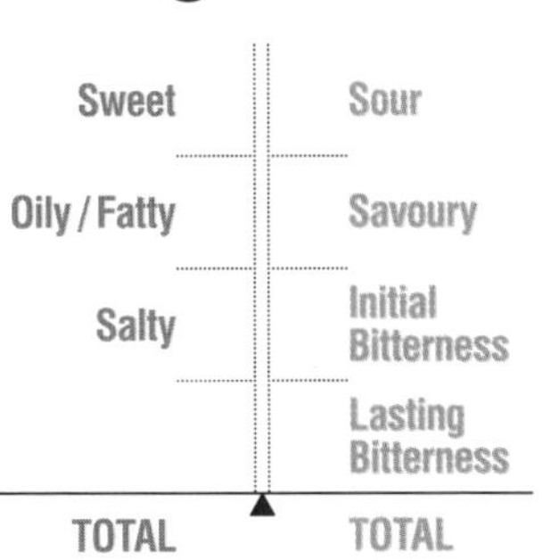

FEEL IT

Warming	Drying
Body	Carbonated
Smooth	Astringent
TOTAL	TOTAL

OVERALL FLAVOUR BALANCE

GRAND TOTAL (SMELL IT + TASTE IT + FEEL IT) ▲ GRAND TOTAL (SMELL IT + TASTE IT + FEEL IT)

TOTAL FLAVOUR SCORE

RATE IT ★	Never again!		Disappointing		Average		Mm..Mmmm		Yes Yes YES!	
	1	2	3	4	5	6	7	8	9	10

Name

A.B.V.

BEER STYLE

Brewer .... Best Before .... Sampled On ....

SEE IT

Beer Colour	White	Yellow	Gold	Straw	Amber	Red	Brown	Black
	1	2	3	4	5	6	7	8

Head Colour	White		Cream		Coffee
	1	2	3	4	5

Head cling & lacing	Poor				Good
	1	2	3	4	5

Clarity	Cloudy				Clear & Bright
	1	2	3	4	5

Carbonation	Flat				Champagne-like
	1	2	3	4	5

Please add your own notes on significant aromas & flavours overleaf

SMELL IT

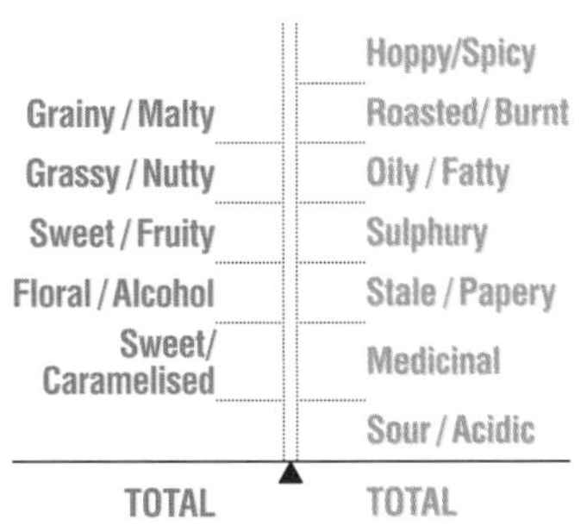

TASTE IT

FEEL IT

Warming | Drying

Body | Carbonated

Smooth | Astringent

TOTAL | TOTAL

OVERALL FLAVOUR BALANCE

GRAND TOTAL (SMELL IT + TASTE IT + FEEL IT) | GRAND TOTAL (SMELL IT + TASTE IT + FEEL IT)

TOTAL FLAVOUR SCORE

RATE IT ★	Never again!		Disappointing		Average		Mm..Mmmm		Yes Yes YES!	
	1	2	3	4	5	6	7	8	9	10

Name

A.B.V.

BEER STYLE

Brewer .... **Best Before** .... **Sampled On** ....

SEE IT

Beer Colour	White	Yellow	Gold	Straw	Amber	Red	Brown	Black
	1	2	3	4	5	6	7	8

Head Colour	White		Cream		Coffee
	1	2	3	4	5

Head cling & lacing	Poor				Good
	1	2	3	4	5

Clarity	Cloudy			Clear & Bright	
	1	2	3	4	5

Carbonation	Flat			Champagne-like	
	1	2	3	4	5

Please add your own notes on significant aromas & flavours overleaf

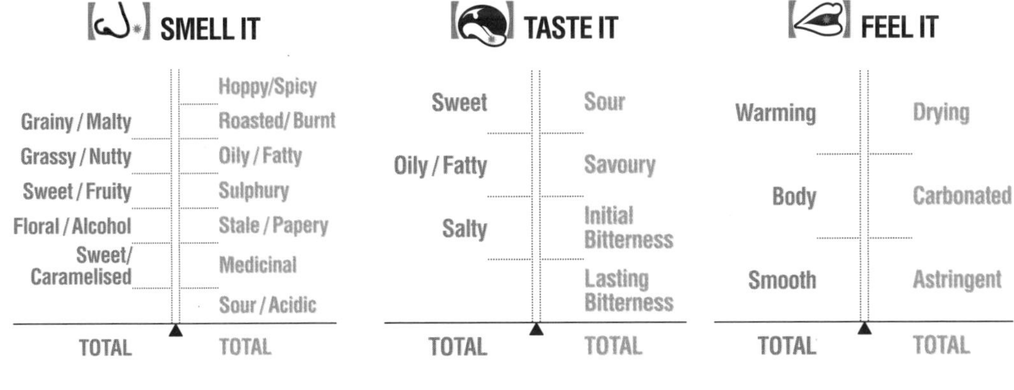

OVERALL FLAVOUR BALANCE

GRAND TOTAL (SMELL IT + TASTE IT + FEEL IT) ▲ GRAND TOTAL (SMELL IT + TASTE IT + FEEL IT)

TOTAL FLAVOUR SCORE

RATE IT ★	Never again!		Disappointing		Average		Mm..Mmmm		Yes Yes YES!	
	1	2	3	4	5	6	7	8	9	10

lame

A.B.V.

BEER STYLE

rewer .... **Best Before** .... **Sampled On** ....

SEE IT

eer Colour	White	Yellow	Gold	Straw	Amber	Red	Brown	Black
	1	2	3	4	5	6	7	8

lead Colour	White		Cream		Coffee
	1	2	3	4	5

Head cling & lacing	Poor				Good
	1	2	3	4	5

larity	Cloudy				Clear & Bright
	1	2	3	4	5

Carbonation	Flat				Champagne-like
	1	2	3	4	5

Please add your own notes on significant aromas & flavours overleaf

SMELL IT

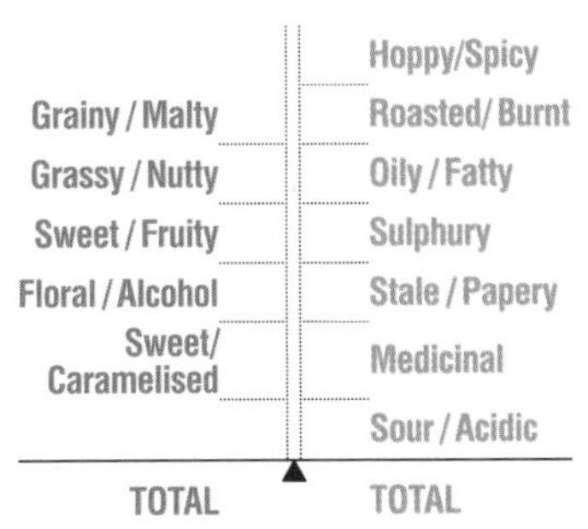

TASTE IT

FEEL IT

Warming	Drying
Body	Carbonated
Smooth	Astringent
TOTAL	TOTAL

OVERALL FLAVOUR BALANCE

GRAND TOTAL (SMELL IT + TASTE IT + FEEL IT) | GRAND TOTAL (SMELL IT + TASTE IT + FEEL IT)

TOTAL FLAVOUR SCORE

RATE IT ★	Never again!		Disappointing		Average		Mm..Mmmm		Yes Yes YES!	
	1	2	3	4	5	6	7	8	9	10

Name

A.B.V.

BEER STYLE

Brewer .... **Best Before** .... **Sampled On** ....

SEE IT

Beer Colour	White	Yellow	Gold	Straw	Amber	Red	Brown	Black
	1	2	3	4	5	6	7	8

Head Colour	White		Cream		Coffee
	1	2	3	4	5

Head cling & lacing	Poor				Good
	1	2	3	4	5

Clarity	Cloudy				Clear & Bright
	1	2	3	4	5

Carbonation	Flat				Champagne-like
	1	2	3	4	5

Please add your own notes on significant aromas & flavours overleaf

OVERALL FLAVOUR BALANCE

GRAND TOTAL (SMELL IT + TASTE IT + FEEL IT) ▲ GRAND TOTAL (SMELL IT + TASTE IT + FEEL IT)

TOTAL FLAVOUR SCORE

RATE IT ★	Never again!		Disappointing		Average		Mm..Mmmm		Yes Yes YES!	
	1	2	3	4	5	6	7	8	9	10

ıme | A.B.V.
BEER STYLE

ewer .... Best Before .... Sampled On ....

SEE IT

er Colour	White	Yellow	Gold	Straw	Amber	Red	Brown	Black
	1	2	3	4	5	6	7	8

ead Colour	White		Cream		Coffee
	1	2	3	4	5

Head cling & lacing	Poor				Good
	1	2	3	4	5

arity	Cloudy				Clear & Bright
	1	2	3	4	5

Carbonation	Flat				Champagne-like
	1	2	3	4	5

Please add your own notes on significant aromas & flavours overleaf

SMELL IT

Grainy / Malty	Hoppy/Spicy
Grassy / Nutty	Roasted/ Burnt
Sweet / Fruity	Oily / Fatty
Floral / Alcohol	Sulphury
Sweet/ Caramelised	Stale / Papery
	Medicinal
	Sour / Acidic
TOTAL	TOTAL

TASTE IT

Sweet	Sour
Oily / Fatty	Savoury
Salty	Initial Bitterness
	Lasting Bitterness
TOTAL	TOTAL

FEEL IT

Warming	Drying
Body	Carbonated
Smooth	Astringent
TOTAL	TOTAL

OVERALL FLAVOUR BALANCE

GRAND TOTAL (SMELL IT + TASTE IT + FEEL IT) | GRAND TOTAL (SMELL IT + TASTE IT + FEEL IT)

TOTAL FLAVOUR SCORE

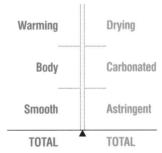

ATE IT ★	Never again!		Disappointing		Average		Mm..Mmmm		Yes Yes YES!	
	1	2	3	4	5	6	7	8	9	10

Name	A.B.V.
BEER STYLE

Brewer .... Best Before .... Sampled On ....

SEE IT

Beer Colour	White	Yellow	Gold	Straw	Amber	Red	Brown	Black
	1	2	3	4	5	6	7	8

Head Colour	White		Cream		Coffee
	1	2	3	4	5

Head cling & lacing	Poor				Good
	1	2	3	4	5

Clarity	Cloudy			Clear & Bright	
	1	2	3	4	5

Carbonation	Flat			Champagne-like	
	1	2	3	4	5

Please add your own notes on significant aromas & flavours overleaf

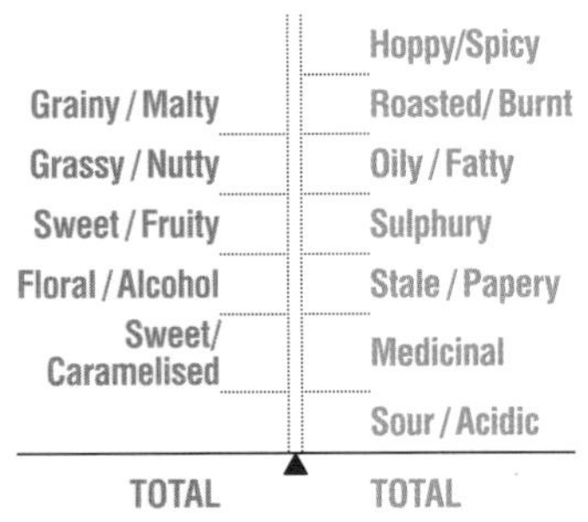

SMELL IT

	Hoppy/Spicy
Grainy / Malty	Roasted/ Burnt
Grassy / Nutty	Oily / Fatty
Sweet / Fruity	Sulphury
Floral / Alcohol	Stale / Papery
Sweet/ Caramelised	Medicinal
	Sour / Acidic
TOTAL	TOTAL

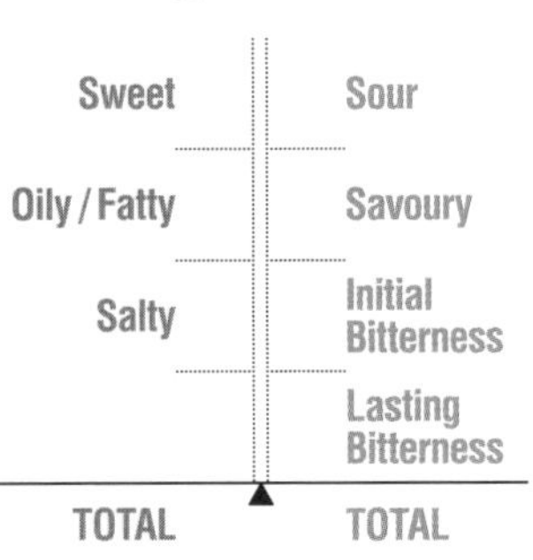

TASTE IT

Sweet	Sour
Oily / Fatty	Savoury
Salty	Initial Bitterness
	Lasting Bitterness
TOTAL	TOTAL

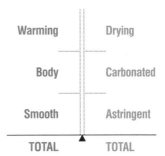

FEEL IT

Warming	Drying
Body	Carbonated
Smooth	Astringent
TOTAL	TOTAL

OVERALL FLAVOUR BALANCE

GRAND TOTAL	GRAND TOTAL
(SMELL IT + TASTE IT + FEEL IT)	(SMELL IT + TASTE IT + FEEL IT)

TOTAL FLAVOUR SCORE

RATE IT ★	Never again!		Disappointing		Average		Mm..Mmmm		Yes Yes YES!	
	1	2	3	4	5	6	7	8	9	10

Name	A.B.V.
	BEER STYLE

Brewer .... Best Before .... Sampled On ....

SEE IT

Beer Colour	White	Yellow	Gold	Straw	Amber	Red	Brown	Black
	1	2	3	4	5	6	7	8

Head Colour	White		Cream		Coffee
	1	2	3	4	5

Head cling & lacing	Poor				Good
	1	2	3	4	5

Clarity	Cloudy				Clear & Bright
	1	2	3	4	5

Carbonation	Flat				Champagne-like
	1	2	3	4	5

Please add your own notes on significant aromas & flavours overleaf

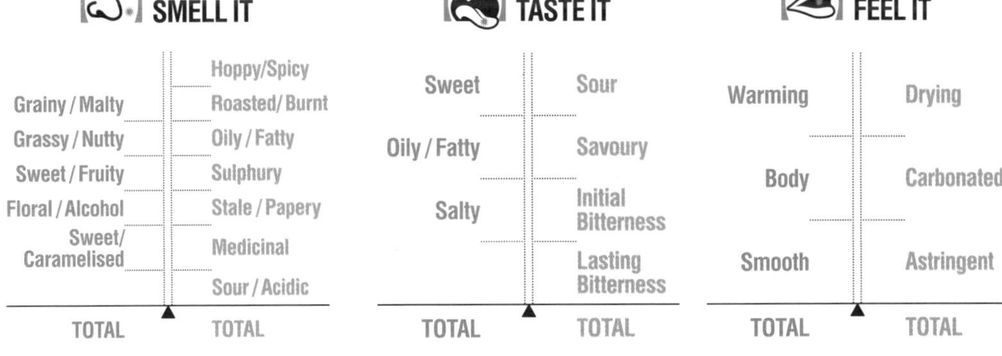

OVERALL FLAVOUR BALANCE

GRAND TOTAL (SMELL IT + TASTE IT + FEEL IT) | GRAND TOTAL (SMELL IT + TASTE IT + FEEL IT)

TOTAL FLAVOUR SCORE

RATE IT ★	Never again!		Disappointing		Average		Mm..Mmmm		Yes Yes YES!	
	1	2	3	4	5	6	7	8	9	10

Name		A.B.V.
		BEER STYLE

Brewer .... Best Before .... Sampled On ....

SEE IT

Beer Colour	White	Yellow	Gold	Straw	Amber	Red	Brown	Black
	1	2	3	4	5	6	7	8

Head Colour	White		Cream		Coffee
	1	2	3	4	5

Head cling & lacing	Poor				Good
	1	2	3	4	5

Clarity	Cloudy				Clear & Bright
	1	2	3	4	5

Carbonation	Flat				Champagne-like
	1	2	3	4	5

Please add your own notes on significant aromas & flavours overleaf

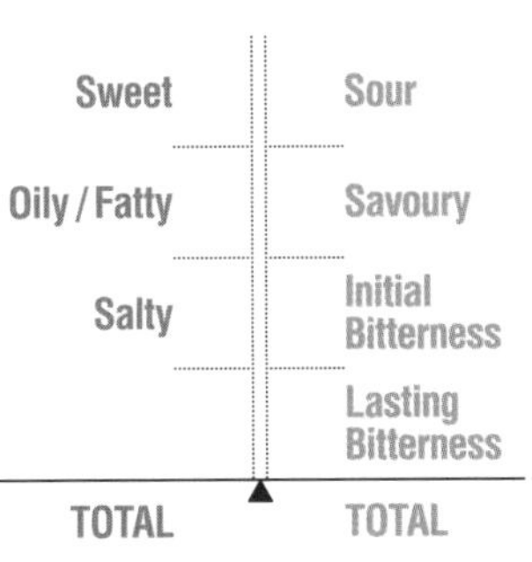

SMELL IT

Grainy / Malty	Hoppy/Spicy
Grassy / Nutty	Roasted/ Burnt
Sweet / Fruity	Oily / Fatty
Floral / Alcohol	Sulphury
Sweet/ Caramelised	Stale / Papery
	Medicinal
	Sour / Acidic
TOTAL	TOTAL

TASTE IT

Sweet	Sour
Oily / Fatty	Savoury
Salty	Initial Bitterness
	Lasting Bitterness
TOTAL	TOTAL

FEEL IT

Warming	Drying
Body	Carbonated
Smooth	Astringent
TOTAL	TOTAL

OVERALL FLAVOUR BALANCE

GRAND TOTAL	GRAND TOTAL
(SMELL IT + TASTE IT + FEEL IT)	(SMELL IT + TASTE IT + FEEL IT)

TOTAL FLAVOUR SCORE

RATE IT ★	Never again!		Disappointing		Average		Mm..Mmmm		Yes Yes YES!	
	1	2	3	4	5	6	7	8	9	10

Name

A.B.V.

BEER STYLE

Brewer .... **Best Before** .... **Sampled On** ....

SEE IT

Beer Colour	White	Yellow	Gold	Straw	Amber	Red	Brown	Black
	1	2	3	4	5	6	7	8

Head Colour	White		Cream		Coffee
	1	2	3	4	5

Head cling & lacing	Poor				Good
	1	2	3	4	5

Clarity	Cloudy				Clear & Bright
	1	2	3	4	5

Carbonation	Flat				Champagne-like
	1	2	3	4	5

Please add your own notes on significant aromas & flavours overleaf

SMELL IT

	Hoppy/Spicy
Grainy / Malty	Roasted / Burnt
Grassy / Nutty	Oily / Fatty
Sweet / Fruity	Sulphury
Floral / Alcohol	Stale / Papery
Sweet/ Caramelised	Medicinal
	Sour / Acidic
TOTAL ▲	TOTAL

TASTE IT

Sweet	Sour
Oily / Fatty	Savoury
Salty	Initial Bitterness
	Lasting Bitterness
TOTAL ▲	TOTAL

FEEL IT

Warming	Drying
Body	Carbonated
Smooth	Astringent
TOTAL ▲	TOTAL

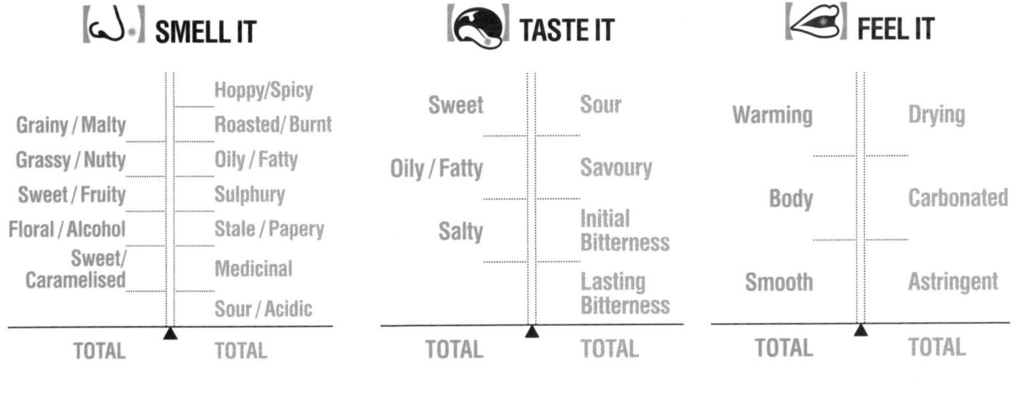

OVERALL FLAVOUR BALANCE

GRAND TOTAL (SMELL IT + TASTE IT + FEEL IT) ▲ GRAND TOTAL (SMELL IT + TASTE IT + FEEL IT)

TOTAL FLAVOUR SCORE

RATE IT ★	Never again!		Disappointing		Average		Mm..Mmmm		Yes Yes YES!	
	1	2	3	4	5	6	7	8	9	10

Name | A.B.V.
BEER STYLE

Brewer | Best Before | Sampled On

SEE IT

Beer Colour	White	Yellow	Gold	Straw	Amber	Red	Brown	Black
	1	2	3	4	5	6	7	8

Head Colour	White		Cream		Coffee
	1	2	3	4	5

Head cling & lacing	Poor				Good
	1	2	3	4	5

Clarity	Cloudy				Clear & Bright
	1	2	3	4	5

Carbonation	Flat				Champagne-like
	1	2	3	4	5

Please add your own notes on significant aromas & flavours overleaf

SMELL IT

Grainy / Malty
Grassy / Nutty
Sweet / Fruity
Floral / Alcohol
Sweet/ Caramelised

Hoppy/Spicy
Roasted/ Burnt
Oily / Fatty
Sulphury
Stale / Papery
Medicinal
Sour / Acidic

TOTAL | TOTAL

TASTE IT

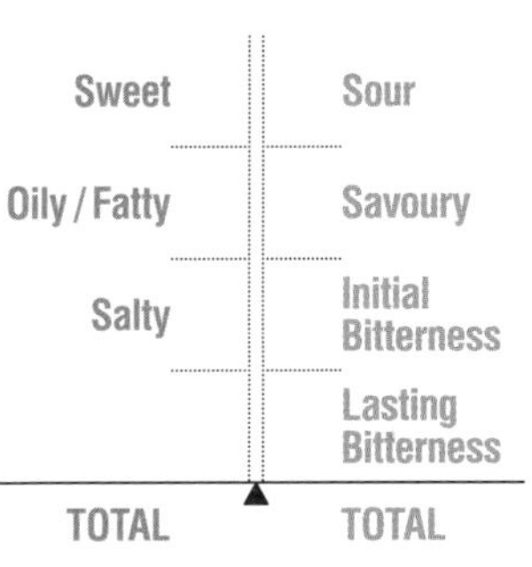

Sweet
Oily / Fatty
Salty

Sour
Savoury
Initial Bitterness
Lasting Bitterness

TOTAL | TOTAL

FEEL IT

Warming
Body
Smooth

Drying
Carbonated
Astringent

TOTAL | TOTAL

OVERALL FLAVOUR BALANCE

GRAND TOTAL (SMELL IT + TASTE IT + FEEL IT) | GRAND TOTAL (SMELL IT + TASTE IT + FEEL IT)

TOTAL FLAVOUR SCORE

RATE IT ★	Never again!		Disappointing		Average		Mm..Mmmm		Yes Yes YES!	
	1	2	3	4	5	6	7	8	9	10

Name

A.B.V.

BEER STYLE

Brewer **Best Before** **Sampled On**

SEE IT

Beer Colour	White	Yellow	Gold	Straw	Amber	Red	Brown	Black
	1	2	3	4	5	6	7	8

Head Colour	White		Cream		Coffee
	1	2	3	4	5

Head cling & lacing	Poor				Good
	1	2	3	4	5

Clarity	Cloudy				Clear & Bright
	1	2	3	4	5

Carbonation	Flat				Champagne-like
	1	2	3	4	5

Please add your own notes on significant aromas & flavours overleaf

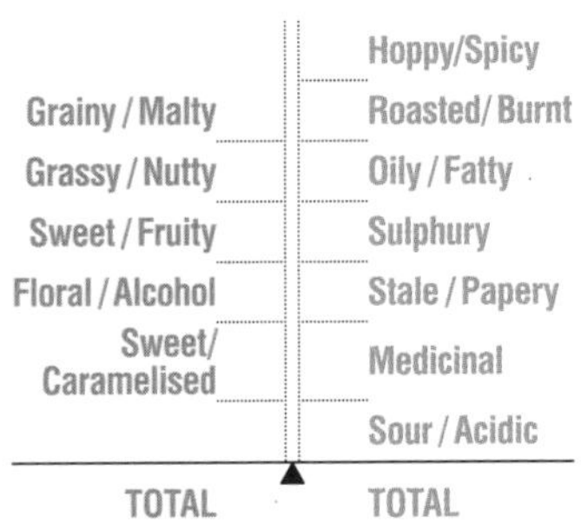

SMELL IT

Grainy / Malty	Hoppy/Spicy
Grassy / Nutty	Roasted/ Burnt
Sweet / Fruity	Oily / Fatty
Floral / Alcohol	Sulphury
Sweet/ Caramelised	Stale / Papery
	Medicinal
	Sour / Acidic
TOTAL	TOTAL

TASTE IT

Sweet	Sour
Oily / Fatty	Savoury
Salty	Initial Bitterness
	Lasting Bitterness
TOTAL	TOTAL

FEEL IT

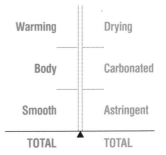

Warming	Drying
Body	Carbonated
Smooth	Astringent
TOTAL	TOTAL

OVERALL FLAVOUR BALANCE

GRAND TOTAL (SMELL IT + TASTE IT + FEEL IT) ▲ GRAND TOTAL (SMELL IT + TASTE IT + FEEL IT)

TOTAL FLAVOUR SCORE

RATE IT ★	Never again!		Disappointing		Average		Mm..Mmmm		Yes Yes YES!	
	1	2	3	4	5	6	7	8	9	10

Name **A.B.V.**
BEER STYLE

Brewer .... **Best Before** .... **Sampled On** ....

SEE IT

Beer Colour	White	Yellow	Gold	Straw	Amber	Red	Brown	Black
	1	2	3	4	5	6	7	8

Head Colour	White		Cream		Coffee
	1	2	3	4	5

Head cling & lacing	Poor				Good
	1	2	3	4	5

Clarity	Cloudy				Clear & Bright
	1	2	3	4	5

Carbonation	Flat				Champagne-like
	1	2	3	4	5

Please add your own notes on significant aromas & flavours overleaf

SMELL IT

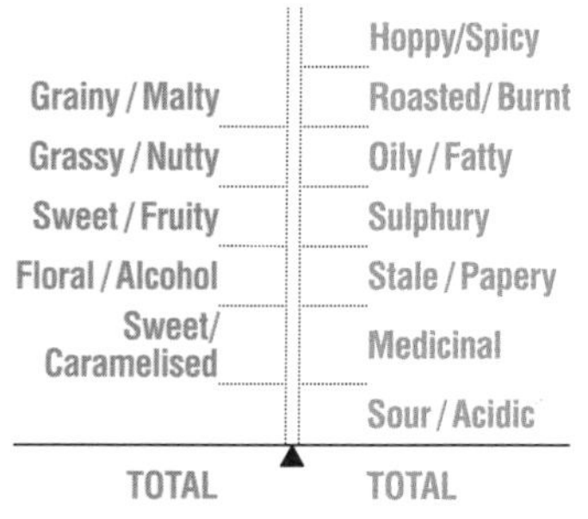

TASTE IT

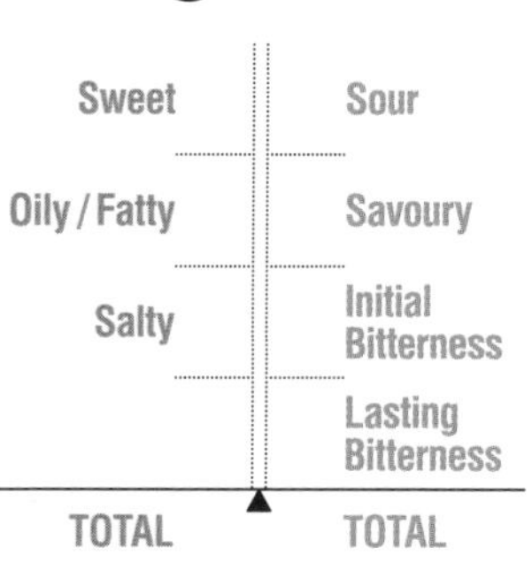

FEEL IT

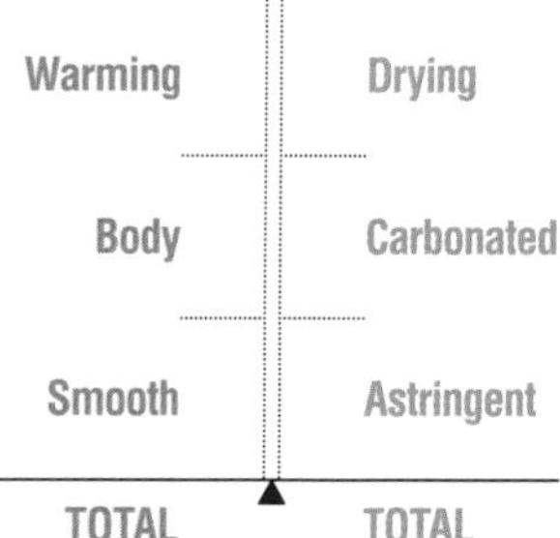

OVERALL FLAVOUR BALANCE

GRAND TOTAL (SMELL IT + TASTE IT + FEEL IT) ▲ GRAND TOTAL (SMELL IT + TASTE IT + FEEL IT)

TOTAL FLAVOUR SCORE

RATE IT ★	Never again!		Disappointing		Average		Mm..Mmmm		Yes Yes YES!	
	1	2	3	4	5	6	7	8	9	10

Name

A.B.V.

BEER STYLE

Brewer ________ Best Before ________ Sampled On ________

SEE IT

Beer Colour	White	Yellow	Gold	Straw	Amber	Red	Brown	Black
	1	2	3	4	5	6	7	8

Head Colour	White		Cream		Coffee
	1	2	3	4	5

Head cling & lacing	Poor				Good
	1	2	3	4	5

Clarity	Cloudy				Clear & Bright
	1	2	3	4	5

Carbonation	Flat				Champagne-like
	1	2	3	4	5

Please add your own notes on significant aromas & flavours overleaf

SMELL IT

	Hoppy/Spicy
Grainy / Malty	Roasted/ Burnt
Grassy / Nutty	Oily / Fatty
Sweet / Fruity	Sulphury
Floral / Alcohol	Stale / Papery
Sweet/ Caramelised	Medicinal
	Sour / Acidic
TOTAL	TOTAL

TASTE IT

Sweet	Sour
Oily / Fatty	Savoury
Salty	Initial Bitterness
	Lasting Bitterness
TOTAL	TOTAL

FEEL IT

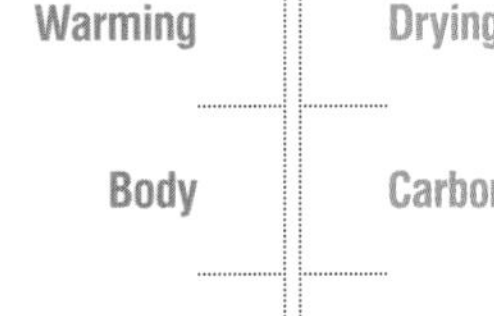

Warming	Drying
Body	Carbonated
Smooth	Astringent
TOTAL	TOTAL

OVERALL FLAVOUR BALANCE

GRAND TOTAL (SMELL IT + TASTE IT + FEEL IT) — GRAND TOTAL (SMELL IT + TASTE IT + FEEL IT)

TOTAL FLAVOUR SCORE

RATE IT ★	Never again!		Disappointing		Average		Mm..Mmmm		Yes Yes YES!	
	1	2	3	4	5	6	7	8	9	10

Schneider Weisse

A.B.V. 5.4%
SERVING TEMP 5–7°C

STYLE Hefe Weizenbier (Yeast Wheatbeer)

BREWER G. Schneider & Sohn

BRAND BACKGROUND In Munich in 1872, Georg Schneider I purchased the rights to brew Wheat beer from King Ludwig II of Bavaria. Everyone else had to adhere to Reinheitsgebot beer laws, except the King, who could brew and drink what he liked.

Though the brewing is now in Kelheim, Schneider maintain the recipe is unchanged since.

OVERALL IMPRESSION A classic Weisse-style Wheat beer, well-balanced, refreshingly fruity and deceptively easy to drink. Watch out, its 5.4% ABV!

BUILDING BLOCKS

WATER	Pure soft water from the Jura mountains.
MALT	40% Barley malt.
HOPS	Moderate addition of German Hallertau hops.
YEAST	Schneider's own top-fermenting Ale yeast.
OTHERS	60% Wheat malt.

SENSE IT

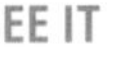

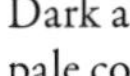

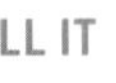

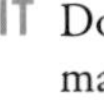
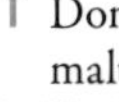
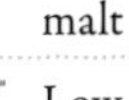

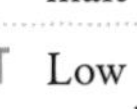
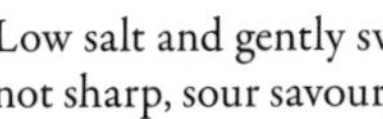
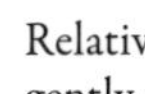

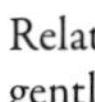
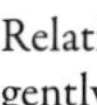

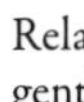
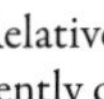
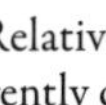

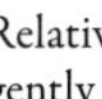

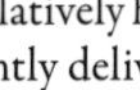
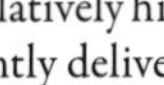
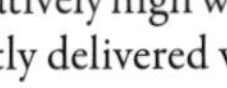
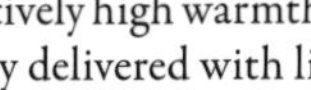
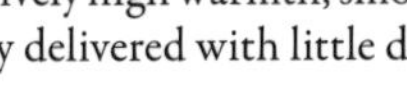
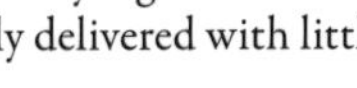
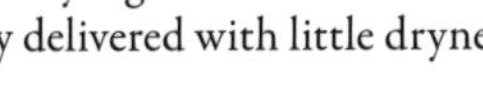
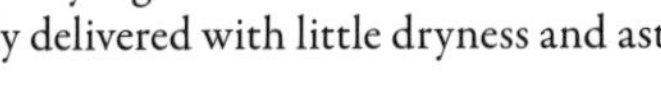

SEE IT	Dark amber and opaque with yeast and proteins, it is highly carbonated with a thick pale coffee-coloured head.
SMELL IT	Dominated by clove-like spiciness, banana, pear drop and lemon fruitiness. Caramel malt aroma softens the light roast coffee, medicinal and acidic notes.
TASTE IT	Low salt and gently sweet with low bitterness. The balance favours a refreshing, but not sharp, sour savoury taste.
FEEL IT	Relatively high warmth, smoothness and medium-low body. Carbonation is high, but gently delivered with little dryness and astringency.

ALE

Schneider Weisse

A.B.V. 5.4%
SERVING TEMP 5–7°C

SEE IT

Beer Colour	White	Yellow	Gold	Straw	Amber	Red	Brown	Black
	1	2	3	4	(5)	6	7	8

Head Colour	White		Cream		Coffee
	1	2	3	(4)	5

Head cling & lacing	Poor				Good
	1	(2)	3	4	5

Clarity	Cloudy			Clear & Bright	
	1	(2)	3	4	5

Carbonation	Flat			Champagne-like	
	1	2	3	(4)	5

SMELL IT

		3	Hoppy/Spicy
Grainy / Malty	3	1	Roasted/ Burnt
Grassy / Nutty	1	0	Oily / Fatty
Sweet / Fruity	3	0	Sulphury
Floral / Alcohol	2	1	Stale / Papery
Sweet/ Caramelised	1.5	3	Medicinal
		2	Sour / Acidic
TOTAL	10.5	10	TOTAL

TASTE IT

Sweet	2.5	3	Sour
Oily / Fatty	0	2	Savoury
Salty	1	2	Initial Bitterness
		1	Lasting Bitterness
TOTAL	3.5	8	TOTAL

FEEL IT

Warming	3.5	0	Drying
Body	2	4.5	Carbonated
Smooth	3	1	Astringent
TOTAL	8.5	5.5	TOTAL

OVERALL FLAVOUR BALANCE

22.5	GRAND TOTAL (SMELL IT + TASTE IT + FEEL IT)	GRAND TOTAL (SMELL IT + TASTE IT + FEEL IT)	23.5

TOTAL FLAVOUR SCORE

46

Worthington's White Shield

A.B.V. 5.6%
SERVING TEMP 10–14°C

STYLE India Pale Ale

BREWER White Shield Brewery (owned by Coors)

BRAND BACKGROUND Hopped up and high in gravity, IPA's were originally destined for the long journey around Africa to India. The sale in Liverpool of IPA casks, salvaged from a shipwreck in the Irish Channel in 1827, ensured British residents got the taste for IPA too. Continuously brewed since 1829, White Shield is the real deal. Still brewed in Burton-on-Trent, the spiritual home of all Pale Ales, it is bottle conditioned allowing it to keep and mature, like a fine wine.

OVERALL IMPRESSION Big flavoured beer from the old school. Every ingredient plays it's part with intense hop, malt and yeast aromas, full-bodied, warm, salty and sweet with a bitterness that goes on and on.

BUILDING BLOCKS

WATER	Hard Burton water, high in Gypsum, from bore-holes on the brewery site.
MALT	Pale Ale and Crystal.
HOPS	Large quantities of Northdown, Goldings and Fuggles cone hops.
YEAST	Fermented with Worthington's original dual yeast strains, it is sterile filtered then re-seeded with fresh yeast before bottling.

SENSE IT

SEE IT Poured with care, so as not to disturb the yeast sediment, it has a bright and lively amber body with a full and lasting crown of cream-coloured foam.

SMELL IT A real nose-full! Rammed with spicy hops, red apples, bananas and pear drops, liquorice, chocolate, malty caramel, liqueur-like alcohol and the odd struck match.

TASTE IT Initially salty and sweet, the bitterness gradually builds and takes hold for a long long lasting finish.

FEEL IT Big on mouthfeel too, White Shield scores in every box with even matches of smooth and astringent, body and carbonation but more warm than drying overall.

Worthington's White Shield

A.B.V. 5.6%
SERVING TEMP 10–14°C

SEE IT

Beer Colour	White	Yellow	Gold	Straw	Amber	Red	Brown	Black
	1	2	3	4	(5)	6	7	8

Head Colour	White		Cream		Coffee
	1	2	(3)	4	5

Head cling & lacing	Poor				Good
	1	2	3	(4)	5

Clarity	Cloudy			Clear & Bright	
	1	2	3	(4)	5

Carbonation	Flat			Champagne-like	
	1	2	3	(4)	5

SMELL IT

		4	Hoppy/Spicy
Grainy / Malty	3.5	1	Roasted/ Burnt
Grassy / Nutty	1	0	Oily / Fatty
Sweet / Fruity	4	2	Sulphury
Floral / Alcohol	2	0	Stale / Papery
Sweet/ Caramelised	2	0	Medicinal
		1	Sour / Acidic
TOTAL	12.5	8	TOTAL

TASTE IT

Sweet	2.5	2	Sour
Oily / Fatty	0	2	Savoury
Salty	3	5	Initial Bitterness
		4	Lasting Bitterness
TOTAL	5.5	13	TOTAL

FEEL IT

Warming	3.5	2.5	Drying
Body	4	3.5	Carbonated
Smooth	3	3	Astringent
TOTAL	10.5	9	TOTAL

OVERALL FLAVOUR BALANCE

28.5	GRAND TOTAL (SMELL IT + TASTE IT + FEEL IT)	GRAND TOTAL (SMELL IT + TASTE IT + FEEL IT)	30

TOTAL FLAVOUR SCORE

58.5

ALE

Draught Guinness WIDGET CAN

A.B.V. 4.1%
SERVING TEMP 6–10°C

STYLE Stout

BREWER Guinness (owned by Diageo)

BRAND BACKGROUND Arthur Guinness bought the brewery at St. James Gate, Dublin in 1759, ceasing Dublin Ale production to concentrate on Porter and Stout in 1799. In the 1800's volumes grew, by export to UK, West Indies, Europe, Africa and America making Guinness the largest brewery in the World at the time. The Harp trademark was registered in 1876. Guinness is now brewed in almost 50 countries.

OVERALL IMPRESSION A definitive Stout, Guinness demonstrates that intense flavours can balance too. Dominated by burnt roast aroma, charcoal dryness and long smooth bitterness.

BUILDING BLOCKS

WATER	Hard liquor. Originally drawn from St. James Springs in the Wicklow Mountains.
MALT	Ale malt.
HOPS	A decent helping of hops from Germany, USA, Australia, new Zealand and the UK.
YEAST	Ale yeast, descended Arthur Guinness' original source.
OTHERS	Flaked barley, Roasted barley

SENSE IT

SEE IT	A trick of the light. Guinness appears jet black but held to a bright light in a thin glass is a dark ruby red, set off with the finest creamy coffee-coloured head.
SMELL IT	Like a serving of double Espresso coffee with burnt toast with underlying touches of struck match, malt, nuts and hops.
TASTE IT 	Once the high salts and low sweetness are done, it's sour, savoury and bitter all the way. The scales tip to the right.
FEEL IT 	The mouthfeel scales tip to the left, with moderate warmth, a big full body and velvety smoothness only partially off-set by moderate dryness and astringency.

Draught Guinness WIDGET CAN

A.B.V. 4.1%
SERVING TEMP 6–10°C

SEE IT

Beer Colour	White	Yellow	Gold	Straw	Amber	Red	Brown	Black
	1	2	3	4	5	6	7	(8)

Head Colour	White		Cream		Coffee
	1	2	3	4	(5)

Head cling & lacing	Poor				Good
	1	2	3	(4)	5

Clarity	Cloudy				Clear & Bright
	1	2	(3)	4	5

Carbonation	Flat				Champagne-like
	(1)	2	3	4	5

SMELL IT

		2	Hoppy/Spicy
Grainy / Malty	2	3	Roasted/ Burnt
Grassy / Nutty	2	0	Oily / Fatty
Sweet / Fruity	1.5	2	Sulphury
Floral / Alcohol	0	1.5	Stale / Papery
Sweet/ Caramelised	1	0	Medicinal
		0	Sour / Acidic
TOTAL	6.5	8.5	TOTAL

TASTE IT

Sweet	1.5	2	Sour
Oily / Fatty	0	2	Savoury
Salty	3	4	Initial Bitterness
		3.5	Lasting Bitterness
TOTAL	4.5	11.5	TOTAL

FEEL IT

Warming	2.5	3	Drying
Body	4	2	Carbonated
Smooth	3.5	2	Astringent
TOTAL	10	6	TOTAL

OVERALL FLAVOUR BALANCE

21	GRAND TOTAL (SMELL IT + TASTE IT + FEEL IT)	GRAND TOTAL (SMELL IT + TASTE IT + FEEL IT)	26

TOTAL FLAVOUR SCORE

47

LAGER

Budweiser

A.B.V. 5.0%
SERVING TEMP 0–4°C

STYLE American Light Lager

BREWER Anheuser-Busch

BRAND BACKGROUND Originating from St. Louis, Missouri in the United States and first brewed in 1876, Budweiser is the World's biggest-selling beer brand. Specially brewed to taste light and 'snappy', it uses a significant amount of rice and beechwood chip maturation process to smooth out the flavour. 'Bud' is brewed in 12 breweries in the US and several more around the Globe.

OVERALL IMPRESSION Rice substituting malt and sparing use of hops ensure no strong flavour traits. Sweet and sour but ultimately smooth, clean and refreshing.

BUILDING BLOCKS

WATER	Soft water.
MALT	Pale Pilsner malt from American barley.
HOPS	Blends of several American and German hop varieties, used sparingly.
YEAST	The original Budweiser Lager yeast.
OTHERS	Rice.

SENSE IT

SEE IT	Crystal clear and very pale yellow, with a sparkling but short-lived bright white head.
SMELL IT	A distinctive drainy-sulphur aroma flashes off in minutes, leaving candied sugar and fresh fruit with only the faintest traces of malt and hop.
TASTE IT	Sweet and sour provide the main balance with very little initial or lasting bitterness.
FEEL IT	High carbonation provides a clean bite. A touch of dryness and no astringency, so ultimately smooth.

LAGER

Budweiser

A.B.V. 5.0%
SERVING TEMP 0–4°C

SEE IT

Beer Colour	White	Yellow	Gold	Straw	Amber	Red	Brown	Black
	1	(2)	3	4	5	6	7	8

Head Colour	White		Cream		Coffee
	(1)	2	3	4	5

Head cling & lacing	Poor				Good
	(1)	2	3	4	5

Clarity	Cloudy				Clear & Bright
	1	2	3	4	(5)

Carbonation	Flat				Champagne-like
	1	2	3	(4)	5

SMELL IT

		1	Hoppy/Spicy
Grainy / Malty	1	0	Roasted/ Burnt
Grassy / Nutty	1	0	Oily / Fatty
Sweet / Fruity	2	2	Sulphury
Floral / Alcohol	1.5	1	Stale / Papery
Sweet/ Caramelised	1	0	Medicinal
		1	Sour / Acidic
TOTAL	6.5	5	TOTAL

TASTE IT

Sweet	3	3	Sour
Oily / Fatty	0	0	Savoury
Salty	1	2	Initial Bitterness
		1	Lasting Bitterness
TOTAL	4	6	TOTAL

FEEL IT

Warming	2.5	3	Drying
Body	2	3	Carbonated
Smooth	4	1	Astringent
TOTAL	8.5	7	TOTAL

OVERALL FLAVOUR BALANCE

19	GRAND TOTAL (SMELL IT + TASTE IT + FEEL IT)	GRAND TOTAL (SMELL IT + TASTE IT + FEEL IT)	18

TOTAL FLAVOUR SCORE

37

LAGER

Pilsner Urquell

A.B.V. 4.4%
SERVING TEMP 6–8°C

STYLE Czech Pilsner

BREWER Plzensky Prazdroj (owned by SAB Miller)

BRAND BACKGROUND In October 1842 Bavarian brewer, Joseph Groll, proudly launched his new beer to the public of Plzen, the World's first golden lager. Subsequently named Pilsner Urquell (the original, from Plzen), all pale lagers are indirectly descended from this beer.

OVERALL IMPRESSION A distinctive beer, befitting the originator of a style. Clearly aromatic, full-bodied and fairly balanced with a long, dry, bitter finish.

BUILDING BLOCKS

WATER Soft water, drawn from local sandstone.

MALT Pale Pilsner malt, malted on site from Bohemian and Moravian barley.

HOPS Heaps of Saaz (German for Zatec) hops, from the nearby Zatec region of Bohemia.

YEAST Pilsner H yeast, traceable back to Groll's original.

SENSE IT

SEE IT Deep straw gold with a fine off-white foam.

SMELL IT Highly aromatic, with Lemongrass, floral, Mint and herbs from the Saaz hops, rich buttery biscuit and caramel aromas from the malt, more flowers, fruit and a light whiff of eggy sulphur from the yeast.

TASTE IT Full-on, with a dose of caramel-sweetness before the powerful and persistent bitterness kicks in.

FEEL IT Every mouthfeel character gets a look-in, with satisfying warmth and rounded body off-set by smooth carbonation and a drying finish. Equal doses of smoothness and astringency ensure the ultimate balance.

LAGER

Pilsner Urquell

A.B.V. 4.4%
SERVING TEMP 6–8°C

SEE IT

Beer Colour	White	Yellow	Gold	Straw	Amber	Red	Brown	Black
	1	2	3	(4)	5	6	7	8

Head Colour	White		Cream		Coffee
	1	(2)	3	4	5

Head cling & lacing	Poor				Good
	1	(2)	3	4	5

Clarity	Cloudy				Clear & Bright
	1	2	3	4	(5)

Carbonation	Flat				Champagne-like
	1	2	(3)	4	5

SMELL IT

		4	Hoppy/Spicy
Grainy / Malty	3	0	Roasted/ Burnt
Grassy / Nutty	2	0	Oily / Fatty
Sweet / Fruity	1	3	Sulphury
Floral / Alcohol	1	1	Stale / Papery
Sweet/ Caramelised	2	0	Medicinal
		0	Sour / Acidic
TOTAL	9	8	TOTAL

TASTE IT

Sweet	3	1	Sour
Oily / Fatty	0	1	Savoury
Salty	1	4	Initial Bitterness
		4	Lasting Bitterness
TOTAL	4	10	TOTAL

FEEL IT

Warming	3	3	Drying
Body	4	3	Carbonated
Smooth	3	3	Astringent
TOTAL	10	9	TOTAL

OVERALL FLAVOUR BALANCE

23	GRAND TOTAL (SMELL IT + TASTE IT + FEEL IT)	GRAND TOTAL (SMELL IT + TASTE IT + FEEL IT)	27

TOTAL FLAVOUR SCORE

50

LAMBIC

Lindemans Kriek

A.B.V. 3.5%
SERVING TEMP 6–8°C

STYLE Fruit Lambic

BREWER Lindemans

BRAND BACKGROUND Originally farmers, the Lindeman family founded their brewery in Brussels in 1809 using their own barley and wheat to brew. Still family owned, Lindemans use open 'coolships' to aerate, cool and pitch the wort with the unique wild yeasts present in the local atmosphere.

Fermentation for 6 months in Oak casks gives a 'young' lambic and 2 years an 'old' lambic. These are blended and given a further 8 -12 month fermentation with Cherry pulp to form the Kriek.

OVERALL IMPRESSION Cherry-fest! A dramatically different beer, with loads of flavour and intense taste sensations, lively, smooth, clean and fantastically fruity.

BUILDING BLOCKS

WATER	Soft water.
MALT	70% Pale Ale malt.
HOPS	Moderate dose of hops, aged for 2 to 3 years, to eliminate bitterness.
YEAST	Brettanomyces Bruxellensis and Lambicus wild yeast, unique to Brussels' Senne valley.
OTHERS	30% Wheat, 'Schaerbeekse' Cherries, Cherry juice, Sugar.

SENSE IT

SEE IT	Re-writes our colour spectrum with an intense cloudy Pink-Red body and rich blushing Peachy-Pink head.
SMELL IT	Initial blasts of Almonds, derived from the Cherry stones, depart to leave intense Cherry fruit aroma, touch of floral acidity and the underlying sweaty barnyard aromas of the original Gueuze.
TASTE IT	Almost entirely a sweet and sour balance, with just a smidge of bitterness.
FEEL IT	At 3.5% it's not warming but is full and smooth with a zingy, uplifting carbonation.

LAMBIC

Lindemans Kriek

A.B.V. 3.5%
SERVING TEMP 6–8°C

SEE IT

Beer Colour	White	Yellow	Gold	Straw	Amber	Red/Pink	Brown	Black
	1	2	3	4	5	(6)	7	8

Head Colour	White		Cream		Peach/Pink
	1	2	3	4	(5)

Head cling & lacing	Poor				Good
	1	(2)	3	4	5

Clarity	Cloudy				Clear & Bright
	(1)	2	3	4	5

Carbonation	Flat				Champagne-like
	1	2	3	(4)	5

SMELL IT

		1	Hoppy/Spicy
Grainy / Malty	1	0	Roasted/ Burnt
Grassy / Nutty	2	0	Oily / Fatty
Sweet / Fruity	4	2	Sulphury
Floral / Alcohol	2	1	Stale / Papery
Sweet/ Caramelised	1	2	Medicinal
		3	Sour / Acidic
TOTAL	10	9	TOTAL

TASTE IT

Sweet	4	3	Sour
Oily / Fatty	0	1	Savoury
Salty	1	2	Initial Bitterness
		1	Lasting Bitterness
TOTAL	5	7	TOTAL

FEEL IT

Warming	2	1.5	Drying
Body	3	3.5	Carbonated
Smooth	4	1.5	Astringent
TOTAL	9	6.5	TOTAL

OVERALL FLAVOUR BALANCE

24	GRAND TOTAL (SMELL IT + TASTE IT + FEEL IT)	GRAND TOTAL (SMELL IT + TASTE IT + FEEL IT)	22.5

TOTAL FLAVOUR SCORE

46.5